people
friendly
food

dairy-free | gluten-free | egg-free | soy-free | nut-free

Erin Paulson & Dana Meroniuk

2 Clever Cooks

Calgary, Alberta

People Friendly Food
Text copyright © 2009 Erin Paulson and Dana Meroniuk
Photographs copyright © 2009 francesfoto
Cover and text design copyright © Jennifer Airhart

Library and Archives Canada Cataloguing in Publication

Paulson, Erin
    People friendly food : gluten-free, dairy-free, egg-free, nut-free,
soy-free / Erin Paulson & Dana Meroniuk.

Includes index.
ISBN 978-0-9865190-0-0

    1. Food allergy--Diet therapy--Recipes. 2. Cookery. I. Meroniuk,
Dana II. Title.

RC588.D53P38 2010   641.5'6318   C2010-902107-X

Disclaimer
The recipes in this book have been carefully tested. To the best of our knowledge, they are safe and nutritious. All the recipes are free of the listed allergens (gluten, dairy, eggs, nuts, and soy), or have suggested alternatives. Please note that some products used in our recipes may contain allergens, depending on the brand. Always read the label to ensure a product is free of the ingredients you are trying to avoid.

All recipes in this book are used at the consumer's risk. The authors expressly disclaim any responsibility for any liability, loss, or risk, personal or otherwise, which is incurred as a consequence, directly or indirectly, of the use and application of any of the contents of this book. Consumers with questions or concerns about their dietary requirements should consult a health professional before using any of these recipes.

Design:	airh[art]design (Jen Airhart)
Photography:	photography by Christina (plus) Nathan
	www.christinaplusnathan.com

Published by:	2 Clever Cooks
Email:	2clevercooks@gmail.com
Website:	www.2clevercooks.com

Printed in Canada

ACKNOWLEDGEMENTS

Thanks to all the people who have made this book possible: our naturopath, Dr. Christine Perkins, for suggesting the idea of the book to Erin; our friend Cathy Brehaut-Snell for helping to test our recipes; our husbands and children for staying out of the way and giving helpful comments and suggestions; all our friends who helped with taste testing – we did occasionally have some pretty bad results before we got good ones; Dana's husband Lee and her Mom Judy for proof-reading – we realize that things that make perfect sense to us don't always make sense to others. Thanks to our designer Jennifer Airhart for her enthusiasm, input, and great work. Finally thanks to our fabulous photographers Christina Robinson and Nathan Krentz of Christina (plus) Nathan for their long hours and passion for the project.

CONTENTS

INTRODUCTION

When we first decided to go ahead and write this cookbook, Dana had recently been diagnosed with several allergies (wheat, gluten, eggs, dairy, beans, legumes, peanuts, and blueberries). Erin had been avoiding her own long list of allergens for many years (wheat, gluten, eggs, dairy, peanuts, sugar, and cabbage). Erin had a definite head-start, especially for baking, and was generous in sharing her knowledge and recipes with Dana. Honestly, some were pretty good, but some were pretty awful (in comparison to what we've developed for this cookbook).

We both love food and cooking, as well as watching cooking shows. We're not afraid to experiment, and believe that's key when adapting recipes to your particular diet requirements. We threw out many experiments along the way (very depressing considering the cost of a lot of our ingredients), but persevered until we discovered the problems and solved them.

We've tried to include helpful tips at the top of each recipe so you don't have to make the same mistakes as us. Be prepared for some failures though, it's how you learn! One thing that we happily discovered is that it isn't quite so important to precisely measure every ingredient as everybody seems to imply (at least, not in these recipes). We both have toddlers (Erin has two), so we don't have the luxury of time and are often approximating measurements with whatever cup or spoon we happen to be holding at the time.

INGREDIENTS AND SUBSTITUTIONS

Many of the processed ingredients we use are not necessarily free of gluten, dairy, eggs, soy, and nuts (it varies by brand). Always read the labels to make sure it meets your dietary requirements. Check out www.celiac.org or www.celiac.com for more comprehensive lists on what contains gluten. Here is a list of some of the ingredients we use that could cause problems:

- Soy sauce (often contains wheat, always contains soy — use the alternate shown in the recipe if you can't have soy)
- Ketchup (often contains malt vinegar which has gluten)
- Worcestershire sauce (may contain gluten)
- Barbeque sauce (may contain gluten)
- Margarine (usually contains whey, so look for lactose-free margarine)

SUBSTITUTIONS

We realize that not all people using this book will need to avoid all of the allergens, so here are some tips for substituting (we have not tried our recipes with these substitutions, but this is what we used as a guideline when removing those allergens from our recipes).

Egg replacer: 1½ teaspoons egg replacer + about 3 tablespoons liquid = 1 egg

Flours: to use regular wheat flour, just add up the total of other flours and starches and use an equal amount of all-purpose flour. You can exclude any xanthan gum if using wheat flour.

Rice milk: use an equal amount of any kind of milk (cow, soy, almond).

Sunflower seed butter: use any nut butter you like, peanut butter being the best substitute.

We have cheese as an optional ingredient in a few of our recipes. For some people who can't tolerate cow's milk cheese, sheep's milk or goat's milk cheese might be ok. Romano cheese is a sheep's milk cheese which is very much like Parmesan cheese.

2 Clever Cooks

A GOOD STARTING POINT –
OUR FAVOURITE RECIPES

These are the recipes that we tend to make over and over again. Mostly because they're fabulous tasting, with not too much effort. For the ones that are a little more effort, they are worth it!

SOUPS & SALADS

CAESAR SALAD DRESSING

This is a fabulous allergy-free version of the old favourite. Make sure everybody eats some or you'll be alienating family and friends with your garlic breath! Try the basil variation – it's fantastic!

⅓ cup canola oil
⅓ cup olive oil
1 or 2 large cloves garlic, minced
1 tablespoon lemon juice
1 tablespoon anchovy paste
1 tablespoon finely ground flax seed
1 tablespoon Dijon mustard

Put all ingredients in the blender and blend for a couple of minutes until they're fully emulsified (the flax, garlic, and Dijon all help to keep the oil and lemon juice from separating).

BASIL VARIATION:
Leave out the anchovy paste; add about a teaspoon of fish sauce (or salt) and a handful of basil leaves.

Makes 1 cup of dressing.

TOMATO, CUCUMBER, AND GARLIC BREAD SALAD

This is the most delicious late summer salad. It's a great way to use up a bountiful harvest of tomatoes – you'll want to make it nightly. The quantities here are just guidelines; do it all to your personal taste.

1 thick slice gluten-free bread, toasted (our Finally Fantastic bread is really good for this)

1 clove garlic, peeled and cut in half

2 tablespoons olive oil

2 tablespoons red wine vinegar

Salt and pepper, to taste

1 extra-large tomato, roughly chopped

6-inch piece of cucumber, roughly chopped

Handful of basil leaves, roughly torn

Handful of mixed greens

Rub toasted bread with the cut side of the clove of garlic and then chop the toast into cubes. If you like a lot of raw garlic, crush or finely chop what is left of the clove and include it in the salad. Mix together garlic (if desired), olive oil, vinegar, salt, and pepper in the bottom of a salad bowl. Add everything else and toss together. Serve immediately.

Serves 2.

TROPICAL CHICKEN SALAD

This makes about double the dressing you need for the salad, so make it again within the next couple of days, or just use the dressing on lettuce. The dressing is fabulous!

SALAD:

1 head romaine lettuce, washed and cut into 1-inch strips

2 chicken breasts, cooked and chopped into bite-sized pieces

1 large papaya, seeded (reserve 2 tablespoons seeds for dressing), peeled, and sliced

1 mango, peeled and sliced

1 large avocado, peeled and sliced

2 green onions, sliced

DRESSING:

½ cup canola oil

⅓ cup agave or honey

⅓ cup rice vinegar

2 tablespoons papaya seeds

2 green onions, chopped

1 teaspoon salt

½ teaspoon dry mustard

Combine salad ingredients in a large bowl. Blend dressing ingredients in the blender for about a minute until the papaya seeds are finely ground. Pour about half the dressing (maybe even less, depending on how heavily you like to dress your salad) over top of the salad and serve immediately. If you're not going to eat all of the salad right away, just dress as much as you will eat.

Serves 4 to 6.

QUINOA SALAD

We never actually use a recipe for this anymore; it becomes one of those "wing-it" type recipes after you've done it a few times. It works well for using up bits of veggies and has lots of pantry items in it so you can almost always make it with what you have at home (assuming you have quinoa!). The spices are just suggestions. If you have something else that you know you prefer, use it. Bottled spice mixes work great also. You can also play with the oil and lemon juice ratio – we like it quite lemony. You may need more or less dressing, depending on how much extra stuff you add. Be creative and use what you've got on hand.

1 cup quinoa
2 cups water

BASE RECIPE:
3 to 4 tablespoons olive oil
3 to 4 tablespoons lemon juice (red or white wine vinegar or rice vinegar also works well)
1 or 2 green onions, sliced (or use a little diced red onion instead)
1 to 3 cups assorted veggies (we like tomatoes, cucumbers, celery, red or yellow bell peppers, and especially avocados)
1 can of salmon or tuna or some leftover meat of any kind (optional)
Salt and pepper, to taste

MEDITERRANEAN VARIATION ADDITIONS:
1 teaspoon oregano
1 teaspoon thyme
¼ cup olives (whatever kind you like)**, pitted and chopped**
¼ cup sundried tomatoes (in oil), sliced
1 tablespoon capers, chopped if large (optional)
Fresh herbs (we use a couple of tablespoons total of dill, basil, and/or parsley if we have them)

MOROCCAN VARIATION ADDITIONS:
¼ cup currants, raisins or dried cranberries
1 teaspoon ground cumin
1 teaspoon ground coriander

Rinse the quinoa thoroughly in a fine mesh strainer under cold water (it has a bitter, soapy tasting coating). Bring the quinoa and water to a boil over medium heat; reduce heat to low and simmer for 15 to 20 minutes until the water is absorbed. Put the quinoa into a bowl; add the rest of the ingredients and mix well. This is good served right away, at room temperature, or cold (although we think it's best slightly warm).

Serves 2 to 4 (depending on how much stuff you add and how hungry you are).

GERMAN POTATO SALAD

This is Erin's favourite potato salad.

6 large potatoes (preferable yellow or red)**, quartered**
½ medium onion, finely chopped
6 thick slices bacon, chopped
1 stalk celery, finely chopped
1 large dill pickle, chopped
1 tablespoon sweet rice flour
½ cup water
¼ cup rice vinegar
1 teaspoon sugar
½ teaspoon salt
½ teaspoon dry mustard
½ teaspoon paprika (smoked if you can find it)

Boil or steam potatoes until tender, about 12 minutes; drain and set aside. Fry onion, bacon, and celery until onion is soft and brown. Add pickle and flour and stir. Add the rest of the ingredients and cook until thickened. Toss gently with the potatoes and serve warm.

Serves 6.

HERBED POTATO SALAD WITH OLIVES AND GREEN BEANS

This is best served warm or at room temperature. It's a great picnic salad as there's no mayonnaise that can spoil. This has quite a strong vinegar flavour when you first make it, so you may want to play with the olive oil to vinegar ratio if you prefer things less tangy. There are also a lot of olives to pit, so you may want to buy them already pitted to save on preparation time.

DRESSING:

½ cup white wine vinegar

¼ cup olive oil

2 tablespoons minced shallots (or red onion)

1 tablespoon chopped fresh parsley

1 tablespoon chopped fresh basil

1 tablespoon chopped fresh dill

2 teaspoons anchovy paste

Salt and pepper, to taste (remember that there are capers and olives added to the salad)

3 cups green or yellow beans (or a mixture of the two), chopped into 2-inch pieces

2 pounds potatoes (preferably red), cut into 1-inch cubes

½ cup chopped red onion (half of that if it's really strong)

½ cup pitted green olives, halved

½ cup pitted black olives (preferably Kalamata), halved

¼ cup drained capers

Mix dressing ingredients together. Cook beans in boiling water for about 5 minutes or until just barely tender; drain and place in a large bowl. Boil or steam potatoes until tender, about 10 minutes; drain and add to bowl with beans. Pour dressing over top and toss. Sprinkle onion, olives, and capers over top.

Serves 8.

2 Clever Cooks

ASPARAGUS AND LEEK SOUP

This is very easy and delicious, but only make it when asparagus is in season or it will be a very pricey bowl of soup. Don't use an immersion blender as it won't purée the soup well enough – you'll be left with stringy bits of asparagus.

1 finely chopped leek (white and pale green part only)
1 clove garlic, minced
1 large bunch asparagus, cut into 1-inch pieces (set aside the tips)
1½ cups chicken broth
Salt and pepper, to taste

Cook the leek and garlic in a little butter or olive oil in a saucepan over medium heat until the leek is soft. Add the rest of the ingredients (except asparagus tips), cover and simmer for 12 minutes. Purée the mixture in a blender until very smooth, pour back into the pan, and add the asparagus tips. Cover and cook on medium heat until the tips are tender, about 5 minutes. Season with salt and pepper.

Serves 2.

CURRIED COCONUT SOUP WITH SPINACH AND MUSHROOMS

This is a light and spicy starter (add cooked rice or rice noodles before serving to make more of a complete meal). Use whatever heat of curry paste you like (yellow is mild, red is medium and green is hot). If you don't have a microplane grater for mincing the lemongrass, you can just leave it in big chunks and bruise it with the back of a knife before you put it in. Take it out just before serving.

¾ cup finely sliced green onions

1½ tablespoons minced fresh lemongrass (use a microplane grater for best results)

1 tablespoon finely grated fresh ginger (again, a microplane grater works best)

2 teaspoons Thai curry paste

5 cups chicken broth

2 cups chopped fresh mushrooms

1 can (14 ounces) coconut milk

1 cup shrimp (or 1 package silken tofu or 1 chicken breast, cut into bite-sized pieces)

3 tablespoons fresh lime juice

Salt and pepper, to taste

1 package (6 ounces) baby spinach leaves

⅓ cup chopped fresh cilantro

Cook green onions, lemongrass, and ginger with curry paste and ¼ cup of broth for a couple of minutes. Add remaining broth, mushrooms, and coconut milk. Bring to a boil and then simmer for 10 minutes. Add shrimp and simmer until cooked through, just a couple of minutes. Add lime juice and season to taste with salt and pepper. To serve, put about ½ cup of spinach and about a tablespoon of cilantro in the bottom of each bowl. Ladle soup into bowls and serve.

Serves 6.

BROCCOLI RED PEPPER SOUP

A nice creamy soup, without the cream. If you can't have any dairy at all, try sprinkling some bacon bits on top instead of the cheese.

1 medium head (about 3/4 lb) broccoli

2 large potatoes (preferably red or yellow)**, chopped into 1-inch pieces**

1 large onion, chopped

1 red bell pepper, chopped

1 large clove garlic, minced

1 teaspoon ground cumin

½ teaspoon dry mustard

2 tablespoons white rice flour

3 cups chicken or vegetable broth

1½ cups grated goat or sheep's milk cheese (optional)

Salt and pepper, to taste

Peel broccoli stem and chop. Separate florets into small pieces and boil or steam until just tender. Rinse with cold water, drain, and set aside. Cook broccoli stems, potato, onion, bell pepper, and garlic in a little butter or oil in a large pot until onion is soft, about 10 minutes. Add cumin and dry mustard, cook another minute. Stir in flour and cook for a couple more minutes until it's evenly incorporated. Add broth and simmer until potatoes are cooked through, about 10 minutes. Sprinkle cheese on top and stir until melted. Season with salt and pepper. Purée roughly with an immersion blender until you have the consistency you like (alternately, scoop out a couple of cups of the soup into a blender, blend until smooth, and then add back to the pot). Stir in the florets and cook over medium heat until heated through.

Serves 4.

SZECHUAN CARROT SOUP

This is a very rich and velvety soup. We love the complexity of the various Asian ingredients.

1 medium onion, chopped

1 stalk celery, chopped

1 clove garlic, minced

1 pound carrots, cut into 1-inch pieces

1 tablespoon finely grated fresh ginger (a microplane grater works well)

½ teaspoon red pepper flakes

3 cups chicken broth

1 can (14 ounces) coconut milk

1½ tablespoons gluten-free soy sauce (or ½ tablespoon each Worcestershire and fish sauce)

1½ tablespoons sunflower seed butter

½ tablespoon lime juice (or to taste)

1 teaspoon sugar

1 teaspoon sesame oil

2 tablespoons chopped fresh cilantro

Cook onion, celery, and garlic over medium heat until soft, about 10 minutes. Add carrots, ginger, red pepper flakes, and broth. Cover and simmer until carrots are soft, about 45 minutes. Stir in remaining ingredients, except for cilantro. Blend mixture in small batches until complete. Use a blender for smoothest result, but an immersion blender or food processor will also work. Reheat soup over low heat until hot. Garnish with cilantro.

Serves 4.

BUTTERNUT SQUASH SOUP WITH COCONUT MILK

This is so simple, but amazing. The fried shallots make it spectacular, but you could use caramelized onions instead.

1 medium butternut squash
1 can (14 ounces) coconut milk
2 to 4 cups chicken broth

½ cup oil for frying
2 shallots, thinly sliced
Salt, to taste

Preheat oven to 350°F.

Split the squash in half lengthwise and remove the seeds. Place it cut side down on a baking sheet and bake for 45 minutes to an hour or until the squash is very soft when poked with a fork. Let it cool for a few minutes until it's easy to handle. Scoop the flesh of the squash into a blender or food processor. Add the coconut milk and 2 cups of chicken broth; blend until smooth. Pour into a large pot and add more chicken broth to achieve the consistency you prefer. Heat over medium heat until hot.

Heat the oil in a small saucepan over medium heat for a couple of minutes. Drop in one slice of shallot to check if the oil is ready – it should immediately bubble furiously. When the oil is ready, drop in enough shallots to have a single layer in the pot (it usually takes us 2 batches to do them all). Let them cook until golden brown and crispy; drain on paper towels and sprinkle with salt. Save the oil for mixing with pasta, rice, mashed potatoes – anything where you'd like some yummy shallot flavour.

Serve the soup and pass around the shallots for people to sprinkle over top.

Serves 4.

SENEGALESE SUNBUTTER SOUP

This soup is a new combination of flavours for most people. We find it gets more addicting with every bite. We often go back for seconds or thirds with this one. This is traditionally finished with peanut butter, but we use sunflower seed butter to make it allergy free. If you can eat peanuts and prefer them, use peanut butter instead.

1 large onion, finely chopped

2 cloves garlic, minced

1 teaspoon cayenne pepper (or to taste - with 1 teaspoon it's medium-hot)

2 tablespoons curry powder

4 cups chicken broth

2 large cans (28 ounce) tomatoes

1 cup sunflower seed butter (Sunbutter brand is really good if you can get it)

1 can (14 ounce) coconut milk

2 tablespoons lime juice

2 tablespoons chopped fresh cilantro

Salt and pepper, to taste

Cook the onion, garlic, and cayenne in a little oil in a large pot over medium heat until the onion softens, about 10 minutes. Add the curry powder and stir to combine thoroughly. Add the broth and tomatoes; simmer for at least 10 minutes, or up to an hour. Add the sunflower seed butter and coconut milk and stir frequently for about 5 minutes or until it has melted into the soup and there are no large clumps left. Blend the soup in batches until smooth (use a blender, immersion blender, or food processor). Add lime juice, cilantro, salt, and pepper just before serving.

Serves 10.

2 Clever Cooks

CREAMY CLAM CHOWDER

The fennel in this makes it unusual and a little richer tasting than most. If you can't find it, you can just leave it out.

1 medium onion, chopped

1 medium head fennel, chopped (optional)

6 thick slices bacon, chopped

2 stalks celery, chopped

3 medium carrots, chopped

6 medium potatoes, chopped

3 cups chicken stock

3 cans (6.5 ounce) clams

1 recipe "Cream" sauce (page 40)

2 teaspoons thyme

2 bay leaves

Salt and pepper, to taste

Fry the onion, fennel, bacon, celery, and carrots in a large deep pot until the onion is soft. Add the rest of the ingredients, bring to a boil, and then simmer until carrots and potatoes are cooked through. Remove bay leaves before serving.

Serves 6.

2 Clever Cooks

ITALIAN WEDDING SOUP

This is super-quick if you have some leftover rice. It's a great all-in-one supper.

6 cups chicken broth
¾ pound Italian sausage
2 medium carrots, sliced
1 cup cooked brown rice
2 cups thinly sliced spinach

Heat broth to boiling in a large saucepan or Dutch oven. Squeeze sausage out of casing into broth as small meatballs. Add carrots and cook for 10 minutes or until carrots are tender. Add rice and spinach; cook for 3 more minutes before serving.

Serves 4.

HAMBURGER SOUP

This is a really comforting winter soup. Like most soups, it just gets better the next day. If you can't find buckwheat you can substitute 1½ cups of cooked rice (preferably short-grain brown rice for the chewy texture).

1½ pounds ground bison, ostrich, or beef

1 medium onion, chopped

3 cups chicken stock

2 cups water

1 large can (28 ounce) tomatoes

4 carrots, sliced

3 stalks celery, sliced

½ cup ketchup

½ teaspoon thyme

1 bay leaf

½ cup buckwheat (the toasted variety is especially tasty)

Salt and pepper, to taste

Parsley, finely chopped

Fry the meat and onions together in a little oil in a large pot (this makes a lot, so make sure you have a big soup pot). Add everything except the buckwheat and simmer for an hour or two. Add the buckwheat and cook about 20 minutes longer or until it is cooked through. Season with salt and pepper and serve with parsley.

Serves 10.

SIDE DISHES

ASPARAGUS WITH GARLIC BREAD CRUMBS

This is quick and yummy.

1 bunch of asparagus

TOPPING:

¼ cup gluten-free bread crumbs

1 clove garlic, minced

½ teaspoon salt

¼ teaspoon pepper

Pinch red pepper flakes (optional)

1 tablespoon butter or margarine, melted

Break the tough ends off the asparagus and discard. Steam or boil the stalks for 5 minutes (3 minutes if they are thin). Drain and spread into a single layer on a shallow baking sheet. Mix together topping ingredients (except butter), then sprinkle evenly over the top of the asparagus. Drizzle with melted butter and then broil for 3 or 4 minutes, until sizzling and starting to brown.

Serves 4 to 6.

ZUCCHINI AND TOMATOES

This is a quick side dish that's great in the summer.

3 medium zucchini, chopped

2 cloves garlic, minced

2 medium Roma tomatoes, chopped

2 tablespoons finely sliced fresh basil

1 tablespoon olive tapenade (or finely chopped olives)

Salt and pepper, to taste

Sauté the zucchini and garlic in a little olive oil over medium heat until lightly browned (5 to 10 minutes). Toss together with remaining ingredients and serve.

Serves 6.

POPCORN CAULIFLOWER

This recipe totally transforms cauliflower. Try it - even if you're not a big cauliflower fan. We think you'll be pleasantly surprised.

1 whole cauliflower, chopped into ½-inch pieces
2 tablespoons olive oil
Salt and pepper, to taste

Preheat oven to 425°F.

Spread the cauliflower in one layer on a sheet pan. Drizzle with the olive oil, sprinkle with salt and pepper. Toss everything around so it's evenly coated. Bake for 15 to 20 minutes, until cauliflower is dark brown in spots.

Serves 4.

ROASTED BEETS

These are great just with a little butter or olive oil, or check out the variations below.

6 medium beets

2 tablespoons butter or olive oil

Salt and pepper, to taste

Preheat oven to 350°F. Wrap each beet individually in foil. Bake for about an hour or until fork tender. Slice or dice, toss with butter or olive oil and salt and pepper.

Serves 6.

BEETS WITH DILL

We like this best served warm or at room temperature.

6 medium beets, roasted and diced

2 tablespoons olive oil

2 tablespoons fresh dill

1 tablespoon rice vinegar

Salt and pepper, to taste

Toss everything together and serve.

Serve 6.

BEETS WITH CARAMELIZED ONIONS

Perfect for a pot-luck or when you have guests. Tastes even better the next day.

2 medium onions, diced

2 tablespoons olive oil

DRESSING:

3 tablespoons olive oil

2 tablespoons apple cider vinegar

1 teaspoon whole grain mustard

Salt and pepper, to taste

6 medium beets, roasted and diced

Sauté onions in olive oil until dark golden brown (about 20 minutes). Combine dressing ingredients together in a blender until emulsified. Mix onions, beets, and dressing together and serve.

Serves 6.

GLAZED CARROTS

This is good when you feel like having something a little more special than plain carrots.

1 pound carrots, sliced
½ cup chicken stock
2 tablespoons butter or margarine
2 tablespoons honey
1 tablespoon fresh dill

Put everything except the dill in a saucepan. Bring to a boil and simmer until carrots are cooked and the sauce coats them. Sprinkle with the dill just before serving.

Serves 4.

COCONUT CURRY SWEET POTATOES

This is great on its own as a meatless meal, but you could also serve it with something light such as fish.

1 large red onion, chopped

1½ tablespoons finely grated fresh ginger

1½ teaspoons ground cumin

1½ teaspoons ground coriander

1 teaspoon salt

½ teaspoon red pepper flakes

½ teaspoon black pepper

1 can (14 ounces) coconut milk

2 tablespoons fish sauce

1½ tablespoons sugar

3 sweet potatoes or yams (about 3 to 3½ pounds), peeled and cut in 1-inch pieces

Heat a little oil over medium-low heat in a large heavy pot. Add onion, ginger, and spices and cook until onion is tender (5 to 10 minutes). Stir in coconut milk, fish sauce, and sugar. Mix well and bring to a boil. Add sweet potatoes and bring back to a boil; reduce heat to low, cover, and cook until potatoes are tender (20 to 25 minutes). Serve with rice.

Serves 6.

SESAME SNOW PEAS AND NOODLES

This is a nice side dish to have with salmon. You can find mirin at Asian markets and some large supermarkets. This is especially good with fresh rice noodles, which you can usually get only at Asian markets – check the ingredients to make sure they don't have any wheat in them (it might just be labelled as starch).

1 tablespoon oil (we like coconut oil, but you can use any neutral oil)

1 tablespoon finely grated fresh ginger

1 clove garlic, minced

1 green onion, sliced

2 tablespoons gluten-free soy sauce (or ½ tablespoon each Worcestershire and fish sauce)

2 tablespoons mirin (Japanese rice wine)

1 tablespoon rice vinegar

1 tablespoon agave or honey

½ tablespoon sesame seeds

½ teaspoon sesame oil

2 cups snow peas, trimmed

4 servings long rice noodles, cooked and drained

Heat a large frying pan or wok over medium heat. Add the oil, ginger, garlic, and green onion and cook for a couple of minutes, stirring frequently. Mix in everything else (except the noodles) and cook for another 3 minutes or so, until the snow peas are crisp-tender. Combine with the noodles and toss to coat.

Serves 4.

GOURMET RICE

A nice change from plain rice.

1½ cups chicken broth

1 cup basmati rice

½ cup finely chopped sweet potato

½ medium onion, finely chopped

½ red bell pepper, finely chopped

1 teaspoon salt

1 teaspoon smoked paprika (or regular paprika if you can't find smoked)

½ teaspoon thyme

½ teaspoon garlic powder

Mix everything together in a medium pot and bring to a boil. Reduce heat, cover, and simmer for 20 minutes or until rice is done to your liking.

Serves 4.

POTATO SIDE DISH VARIATIONS

CRISPY OVEN POTATOES

2 pounds potatoes, chopped roughly into 1½-inch pieces
Olive oil
Salt and pepper, to taste

Preheat oven to 425°F.

Place potatoes on a baking sheet and drizzle generously with olive oil. Sprinkle with salt and pepper. Bake for 15 minutes, mix them up, and bake another 10 to 15 minutes, until brown and crispy.

Serves 4.

CARAMELIZED ONION AND BACON MASHED POTATOES

2 pounds potatoes, quartered
½ pound bacon, chopped
1 medium onion, sliced
Salt and pepper, to taste

Boil the potatoes for about 15 minutes, or until tender; mash potatoes. Fry the bacon and onions together until onions are caramelized and bacon is crisp. Pour the bacon, onion, and bacon fat over the potatoes and mix well. If potatoes are too dry, add a little chicken broth or olive oil to moisten. Season with salt and pepper and serve.

Serves 4.

GARLIC MASHED POTATOES

1 head garlic (8 to 10 medium cloves)
2 pounds potatoes, quartered
⅓ to ½ cup butter or margarine or olive oil (will depend on how dry your potatoes are)
Salt and pepper, to taste

Preheat oven to 350°F.

Chop off the top off the garlic head to just expose the cloves. Place in a small piece of foil, drizzle with a little olive oil, and wrap tightly. Bake for 20 minutes or until fragrant and cloves are soft. Boil the potatoes for about 15 minutes or until tender. Squeeze the garlic out of the skins into the potatoes, add butter or oil, and mash. Season with salt and pepper and serve.

Serves 4.

BOILED AND SMASHED NEW POTATOES

2 pounds small new potatoes
Olive oil
Salt and pepper

Boil the potatoes for about 15 minutes or until tender. Squish the potatoes, one at a time with the bottom of a frying pan to about a 1-inch thickness. Fry in a little olive oil over medium-high heat until brown and crispy. Season with salt and pepper and serve.

Serves 4.

TEMPURA BATTER AND DIPPING SAUCE

This is a light, super crispy batter. It's great with the dipping sauce - if you can tolerate soy. This also makes a great fish batter; just add ¼ teaspoon of garlic salt and a little less club soda.

BATTER:

1¼ cups white rice flour

1 can (12 ounces) cold club soda

ASSORTED VEGETABLES – we like:

Onion rings (sweet onions are best)

Sweet potato or yam, sliced ½-inch thick, then steamed for about 5 minutes

Sweet bell pepper rings

Zucchini, sliced ½-inch thick

1 cup sweet rice flour

Oil for deep frying

Heat oil to 350°F for frying.

Whisk together white rice flour and club soda until it is the consistency of pancake batter. If you have to add flour, add only a tablespoon at a time – it thickens up very quickly.

To make the tempura, first coat the vegetables with sweet rice flour, and then dip in the batter. Gently place into the hot oil; fry until golden. Season with salt and serve with dipping sauce. Make sure to let the oil come back up to 350°F before frying each batch or they will absorb too much oil.

DIPPING SAUCE:

You can find mirin at Asian markets or in the Asian section of some large supermarkets.

½ cup mirin (Japanese rice wine)

½ cup gluten-free soy sauce (preferably tamari, the naturally brewed kind)

2 tablespoons water

1 tablespoon rice vinegar

1 tablespoon sugar or agave (or more, to your taste)

1 teaspoon finely grated fresh ginger

Combine all ingredients in a small saucepan and cook over medium-low heat until sugar is completely dissolved. If you use agave instead of sugar, you can just whisk everything together until combined.

Serves 4 to 6.

2 Clever Cooks

DUMPLINGS

These have a great texture. Masa harina is a fabulous flour for these (you can find it in Mexican markets, or in the Mexican section of some large supermarkets). Make these on top of soup, stew, chili, or whatever you'd like.

¾ cup masa harina (corn flour tortilla mix)

¼ cup rice flour

1 teaspoon baking powder

¼ teaspoon baking soda

¼ teaspoon salt

¼ cup cold butter or shortening, cut into small pieces

½ cup rice milk

Stir together masa harina, rice flour, baking powder, baking soda, and salt in a bowl. Mash in the butter pieces with a fork until crumbly. Add rice milk and stir to combine (do not overmix).

Drop by heaping tablespoons onto simmering soup, leaving a little space between. Reduce heat to low and simmer, covered, until tops of dumplings are dry to the touch, 15 to 20 minutes.

Makes 8 to 10 dumplings.

"CREAM" SAUCE

This is a versatile sauce that can be used as a base instead of cream. You can vary the liquid ingredients based on the final use of the sauce (use broth and a little wine or sherry for a savoury dish, water or rice milk and maybe a bit of liqueur for a sweet dish). You can season to taste after blending.

1⅔ cups liquid (water, broth, wine, rice milk)
⅓ cup white rice (medium grain to long grain is best, short grain can be a bit gluey)

Salt and pepper, to taste
Lemon juice, to taste (optional)

Bring the liquid to a boil; add the rice, and reduce the heat to low. Cover and simmer for about 35 minutes, or until the liquid is almost all absorbed and the rice is very soft. Purée in a blender until smooth. Season to taste, and thin with additional liquid to get the consistency you prefer.

Makes 2 cups.

BEET KETCHUP

This is a really interesting and tasty alternative to tomato ketchup. It goes great on burgers or sandwiches.

1 onion, diced
3 cloves garlic, minced
1 cup agave or sugar
¾ cup red wine vinegar
3 cups cooked diced beets

Sauté the onion and garlic in a little oil until soft. Add the agave and vinegar to warm through (or if you're using sugar, until the sugar is dissolved). Put the beets in a blender; add the warm vinegar mixture and purée until smooth. If the ketchup is not thick enough, simmer until it is the consistency you desire.

MAIN DISHES

CHICKEN WITH COCONUT CURRY SAUCE

This also works great on salmon. It's a great meal for those nights when you don't have much time or energy to cook – the curry is done in the time it takes the rice to cook. We like to measure out the coconut milk before we start, then use what is left in the can as part of the liquid used to cook the rice.

2 boneless, skinless chicken breast halves or thighs
Salt and pepper, to taste

1 large green onion, sliced
2 teaspoons Thai curry paste (we prefer red, which is medium hot)
⅓ cup chicken broth
½ cup coconut milk
1 tablespoon lime juice, or to taste

Chop chicken into bite size pieces and season with salt and pepper. Sauté on medium heat until almost cooked through; transfer to plate. Add green onion and curry paste to the same pan; stir 1 minute. Pour in broth and boil until reduced to glaze (another minute or two). Add coconut milk and cook until sauce coats a spoon, stirring constantly. Mix in lime juice. Return chicken to skillet. Reduce heat to medium-low; simmer until cooked through, about 2 minutes.

Serves 2.

CHICKEN WITH PASSION FRUIT AND MANGO SAUCE

This is delicious, and a great meal to make for company. It's really not difficult at all, but is very impressive. Make sure you use passion fruit juice – it really is a fabulous flavour. We've tried it with other juice mixes and it's just not the same.

4 chicken breasts, chopped into bite-sized pieces

Salt and pepper, to taste

2 cloves garlic, minced

1 tablespoon finely chopped jalapeno (remove the seeds if you don't want it too spicy)

2 cups passion fruit juice

½ cup triple sec or other orange liqueur

2 ripe mangos, diced

1 red bell pepper, diced

4 tablespoons chopped fresh basil or cilantro

1 tablespoon lime juice, or to taste

1 tablespoon cornstarch, dissolved in 2 tablespoons cold water

Season chicken with salt and pepper. Fry chicken in a little olive oil in a large sauté pan for about 5 minutes or until chicken is just a little pink. Set aside on a plate while you make the sauce.

Sauté garlic and jalapeno for about 1 minute in the same pan chicken was cooked in. Add the passion fruit juice, liqueur, mangos, and red pepper and boil for about 10 minutes to reduce the sauce and intensify the flavour. Add the basil or cilantro, and lime juice. Add the chicken back at this point and cook until done. Add cornstarch mixture; cook another minute or so until the sauce is thickened. Serve over steamed rice.

Serves 4.

CHICKEN WITH SPICY SUNBUTTER SAUCE

This sauce is addicting! If you don't care for cilantro, you can either leave it out, or use parsley instead.

1½ lbs chicken breasts

2 cups water

1 green onion, cut in half

1 quarter-sized piece of fresh ginger, crushed

1 tablespoon dry sherry

½ teaspoon salt

½ teaspoon sugar

Place chicken in a medium pan with the rest of ingredients. Bring to a boil, cover, and simmer for 20 minutes. Remove from heat and let stand, covered, until chicken is cool enough to handle. Pull meat into long shreds.

SPICY SUNBUTTER SAUCE:

3 tablespoons smooth sunflower seed butter

⅓ cup canola oil

⅓ cup agave or honey

¼ cup gluten-free soy sauce (or 1½ tablespoons each Worcestershire and fish sauce)

2 tablespoons finely sliced green onion

2 tablespoons finely minced fresh cilantro

1 tablespoon rice vinegar

1 teaspoon sesame oil

½ to 1 teaspoon ground cayenne pepper, to taste

Soba noodles (Eden brand has gluten-free ones), or rice noodles for serving

GARNISH OPTIONS:

Cucumber slices

Shredded carrots

Stir together sunflower seed butter and oil until smoothly blended. Do not add other ingredients until this is done, or you won't get the right consistency. Add remaining ingredients and stir well to blend. The sauce can be used immediately, but it is better if you make it a few hours ahead and allow flavours to combine.

Cook noodles according to package directions, and then rinse with cold water and toss with a little of the sauce. Place chicken shreds on noodles; garnish with cucumber or shredded carrots if desired. Serve additional sauce on the side.

Serves 4.

MOROCCAN CHICKEN

This is a simple dish to throw together in the morning and enjoy when you get home for supper. If you happen to have a Moroccan spice mix, use 1½ tablespoons of it in place of the dried spices.

1 large onion, chopped

4 cloves garlic, minced

1 teaspoon red pepper flakes

1 teaspoon ground cumin

1 teaspoon ground coriander

1 teaspoon ground ginger

1½ pounds skinless bone-in chicken thighs

1½ cups white wine

½ cup raisins

½ cup dried apricots, halved

3 tablespoons honey

1 cinnamon stick

½ teaspoon salt

⅓ cup pitted green olives

Mix the onion, garlic, and spices together. Place the chicken in a slow-cooker; add the onion mixture on top, and then add the rest of the ingredients (except the olives). Cook for 4 hours on high or 8 hours on low. Stir olives in just before serving.

If you don't want to use a slow-cooker, sauté the onions, garlic, and spices in a large pot in a little oil for 5 to 10 minutes or until the onion is soft. Add everything else except for the olives and bring to a boil, then simmer uncovered until the chicken is cooked through (probably about 30 minutes, depending on the thickness of the thighs). If you'd like a thicker sauce, turn the heat up at the end for 10 minutes, or until it is the consistency you like. Stir in olives just before serving.

Serves 4.

CRISPY CHICKEN STRIPS

These are one of our personal favourites. These can be made with Romano cheese (if you can eat sheep's milk cheese), or with garlic and herbs if you can't have any dairy. Either way, they're delicious.

15 chicken tenders or 3 chicken breasts cut in 5 strips each

FLOUR MIXTURE:

⅓ cup rice flour

1 tablespoon egg replacer

½ cup rice milk

COATING:

1¼ cups gluten-free bread crumbs

¾ cup finely grated Romano cheese (or 2 cloves garlic, minced, and 1 teaspoon each dried oregano, basil, and thyme)

½ teaspoon salt (increase to 1 teaspoon if not using cheese)

AVOCADO DIPPING SAUCE:

1 avocado, diced

1 tablespoon fresh dill, chopped

½ tablespoon lemon juice

1 green onion, sliced

Salt and pepper, to taste

Mix the flour together with the egg replacer in a shallow bowl. Pour the rice milk in another bowl. Combine the crumbs, cheese (or garlic and spices), and salt in a third bowl. Dip the chicken first in the flour mixture, then the rice milk, then the bread crumbs, pressing them in so they stick. Heat a large frying pan over medium-high heat and then cover the bottom in oil. Cook the chicken in 2 or 3 batches, for about 3 minutes each side until golden brown and cooked through.

Combine all dip ingredients and mix well until the avocado starts to break down and get creamy.

Serves 4.

2 Clever Cooks

SMOKY CRANBERRY WINGS

This is one of our favourites. It works well with pork as well – chops or ribs. You can also grill the wings first; then pour the sauce over and bake to finish.

SPICE RUB:

2 tablespoons sugar

1 tablespoon smoked paprika

2 teaspoons dry mustard

2 teaspoons celery salt

2 teaspoons garlic powder

2 teaspoons pepper

1 teaspoon onion powder

1 teaspoon salt

1 teaspoon ground chipotle chile powder (optional)

2 pounds chicken wings

SAUCE:

¾ cup cranberry sauce

½ cup maple syrup

¼ cup cranberry juice

2 tablespoons Dijon mustard

1 tablespoon orange liqueur

Salt and pepper, to taste

Preheat oven to 425°F.

Mix spice rub ingredients together, then toss with chicken wings in a Ziploc bag to coat. Bake the wings on a shallow baking pan for 10 to 15 minutes or until the skin starts to get crisp. Whisk together sauce ingredients in a small pot over medium heat until the cranberry sauce melts and the sauce is smooth. Pour sauce over wings and toss them to evenly coat; turn oven down to 350°F and continue baking until wings are cooked through, approximately 20 minutes.

Serves 4.

VIETNAMESE CHICKEN WITH CARROT AND CUCUMBER PICKLE

This is just like the rice vermicelli (bun) dishes you get in Vietnamese restaurants. Chopping the veggies for the pickle goes much faster with one of those fancy slicers (either a Japanese Benriner or a mandolin).

CHICKEN INGREDIENTS:

1 large clove garlic, minced

2 tablespoons sugar

1½ tablespoons fish sauce

1½ tablespoons oil

1 tablespoon lime juice

Asian hot chili sauce, to taste

1½ pounds boneless, skinless chicken breasts, cut into bite-sized pieces

PICKLE INGREDIENTS:

2 medium carrots, peeled

6-inch piece of English cucumber, seeded

½ cup rice vinegar

¼ cup sugar

1 teaspoon salt

SAUCE INGREDIENTS:

Pickle marinade

¼ cup water

Asian hot chile sauce, to taste

4 servings of rice vermicelli, boiled until tender and then rinsed with cold water and drained

GARNISH: **fresh mint and cilantro leaves**

Whisk together garlic, sugar, fish sauce, oil, lime juice, and hot sauce in a large bowl until sugar is dissolved. Add chicken and toss to coat; marinate 15 minutes.

Cut carrots and cucumber into ⅛-inch thick matchsticks (2-inches long). Whisk together vinegar, sugar, and salt in a bowl until sugar is dissolved; then add vegetables and toss to combine. Let stand, until vegetables wilt, about 15 minutes. Drain and reserve the liquid for the sauce. Mix the reserved liquid with the water and hot sauce to make sauce for pouring over the noodles.

Heat frying pan over medium-high heat until hot, add enough oil to cover the bottom of the pan, and then fry chicken in batches, until browned and cooked through, about 5 minutes per batch. (You could also thread these onto skewers and grill until cooked through).

Place rice vermicelli in large noodle bowls and place chicken on top. Serve with the carrot and cucumber pickle, mint, cilantro, and sauce. You can also pass more hot sauce separately for people who would like it spicier.

Serves 4.

TOMATO BASIL PEPPERCORN CHICKEN WITH LINGUINI

This is so yummy! The brandy and basil at the end really make it fabulous. Make sure to toss everything with the pasta in the pan so it really absorbs the flavour. To get a thicker sauce, add a bit of pasta water at the end. The green peppercorns may be difficult to find; some grocery stores carry them, either near the spices or near the pickles (they will be in a can or jar). If you can't find them in the grocery store, try a gourmet cooking shop.

1 small red onion, cut in half lengthwise and then sliced thin

¾ cup chopped tomato

¼ cup thinly sliced sun-dried tomatoes (packed in oil)

1 tablespoon lemon juice

½ tablespoon green peppercorns, drained and chopped

1 large clove garlic, minced

½ teaspoon salt

½ teaspoon pepper

1 pound boneless, skinless chicken breast, chopped in bite-sized pieces

2 tablespoons brandy

2 tablespoons thinly sliced fresh basil

1 pound rice linguini or spaghetti, cooked according to package directions

Stir onion, tomato, sun-dried tomatoes, lemon juice, green peppercorns, garlic, salt, and pepper together in a bowl.

Heat a large frying pan over medium heat; add a little oil and fry chicken pieces until they are almost cooked through. Add the tomato mixture, stir together, and cook for a couple more minutes. Add the brandy and basil, cook another minute or so, and then add the drained pasta to the pan. Stir everything together to coat the pasta thoroughly.

Serves 3 to 4.

THAI CHICKEN PIZZA

Not your typical pizza, but a nice change from the usual. If you can't have any dairy, it's still really good without any cheese.

SAUCE:

½ cup sunflower seed butter

¼ cup water

3 tablespoons rice vinegar

3 tablespoons brown sugar

3 tablespoons gluten-free soy sauce (or 1 tablespoon Worcestershire and ½ tablespoon fish sauce)

1 teaspoon finely grated fresh ginger

1 small clove garlic, minced

½ teaspoon red pepper flakes

1 cup sliced oyster mushrooms (or button mushrooms, if you prefer)

1 small clove garlic, minced

1 tablespoon butter or margarine

Salt and pepper, to taste

1 large chicken breast

½ red bell pepper, chopped

1 green onion, sliced

1 cup goat or non-dairy mozzarella cheese (optional)

2 9-inch pizza crusts (see page 83)

Preheat oven to 425°F.

Whisk together sauce ingredients in a small saucepan and simmer for 5 minutes over medium-low heat. Thin with additional water if it's too thick (it should be about ketchup consistency).

Fry mushrooms and garlic in butter until the mushrooms have released all their liquid and are almost dry again. Season with salt and pepper.

Sauté or grill chicken breast until cooked through. Let rest 5 minutes and then slice thinly. Spread sauce over pizza crusts and top with chicken, mushrooms, red pepper, green onion, and cheese; bake for 12 to 15 minutes.

Makes two 9-inch pizzas.

LETTUCE WRAPS

Delicious, crunchy little bundles. You can also just slice up the lettuce and serve everything over top like a salad if you want a less messy eating experience.

FILLING:

1 pound ground pork, turkey, or chicken

1 small red bell pepper, finely chopped

1 cup shredded carrot

½ cup fresh cilantro, chopped

6 green onions, sliced

1 tablespoon finely grated fresh ginger

1 clove garlic, minced

2 tablespoons fish sauce

2 tablespoons Thai sweet red chili sauce

1 teaspoon sesame oil

SAUCE:

¼ cup sunflower seed butter

¼ cup fresh cilantro, chopped

¼ cup lime juice

2 tablespoons fish sauce

2 tablespoons agave or sugar

1 tablespoon rice vinegar

1 teaspoon coriander

¼ teaspoon red pepper flakes (optional)

½ English cucumber, diced

1 head iceberg lettuce, separated into leaves

Fry the pork in a little oil until almost cooked through. Add remaining filling ingredients and cook for 5 minutes longer, or until carrots are soft.

Mix together sauce ingredients in a small saucepan over low heat and cook until sauce is a smooth consistency.

Serve with lettuce leaves for wrapping and cucumber for sprinkling on top.

Serves 4.

DUBLIN CODDLE

A quick and tasty dinner. Add some chopped kale (at the beginning), or spinach (in the last 5 minutes), to increase the nutritional value. If you can't find celery root (also called celeriac – an ugly, knobby root vegetable that tastes like celery, but has a potato consistency when cooked), you can just use a couple more potatoes or a few carrots, chopped.

3 pounds potatoes, cut into 1-inch pieces

1 celery root, peeled and cut into 1-inch pieces

2 onions, chopped into 1-inch pieces

¼ cup chopped fresh parsley, divided

1 pound breakfast sausage, squeezed out of casings into approximately 1-inch chunks

4 bacon slices, coarsely chopped (optional)

1½ cups water or broth

Pepper, to taste

Place potatoes, celery root, onions, and 2 tablespoons parsley in bottom of a large saucepan. Scatter sausage and bacon over top. Pour water or broth over and season with pepper. Bring to a boil over high heat. Cover pan and reduce heat to medium-low; simmer about 30 minutes, until potatoes and sausage are cooked through. Remove cover from pan, increase heat, and boil until liquid is mostly absorbed. Sprinkle with remaining 2 tablespoons parsley and serve.

Serves 6.

MAPLE SQUASH AND SAUSAGE

This is a simple and surprisingly delicious meal. Use frozen butternut squash to make it even quicker (if you can find it).

1 medium butternut squash
½ pound breakfast sausage
2 tablespoons butter
2 tablespoons maple syrup

Preheat oven to 350°F.

Split the squash in half lengthwise and remove the seeds. Place it cut side down on a baking sheet and bake for 45 minutes to an hour, or until the squash is very soft when poked with a fork.

Fry the sausage over medium heat, breaking it up as you fry it. Scoop the squash out of the skin in chunks, and add to the pan with the sausage (if using frozen squash, just add it in frozen, then put a lid over the pan to help it cook through). Add the butter and maple syrup, and cook until the sausage is done.

Serves 2 to 3.

2 Clever Cooks

SAUSAGE STUFFED ACORN SQUASH WITH MAPLE GLAZE

The maple syrup and sausage make a nice crust on top.

4 small acorn squash

FILLING:

¾ pound breakfast sausage, squeezed from casings

¼ pound smoked garlic sausage, finely chopped

½ cup rice flour

½ cup beef broth

½ cup diced red bell pepper

2 green onions, thinly sliced

½ teaspoon pepper

¼ teaspoon salt

GLAZE:

⅓ cup maple syrup

Preheat oven to 400°F.

Cut the top and bottom off of each acorn squash. Scoop out the seeds and then cut each squash in half, creating two rings. Place squash rings in single layer on a large sheet pan. Mix filling ingredients together and divide evenly among squash rings. Brush the top of the squash and filling with maple syrup. Bake for 35 minutes.

Serves 4.

PORK CHOPS WITH APPLE AND ONION GRAVY

This is just a yummier way of having applesauce with your pork chops - not much more difficult either. We like to serve this with roasted root vegetables – an assortment of potatoes, sweet potatoes, carrots, beets, or parsnips – whatever you have, with an onion. Toss with a bit of oil, salt, and pepper and roast at 375°F until tender.

4 pork chops, ¾-inch thick
Salt and pepper, to taste

1 medium onion, sliced
¾ cup chicken broth
½ cup applesauce
¼ teaspoon ground cinnamon
½ teaspoon balsamic vinegar
⅛ teaspoon garlic powder

Season pork chops with salt and pepper. Brown in a large frying pan on medium-high heat, about 3 minutes on each side; set aside on a plate. Add onion to frying pan and sauté on medium heat until soft and brown, about 10 minutes. Add broth, applesauce, and cinnamon to pan and stir. Place pork chops back in the pan and cook, covered, until pork is cooked through, about 5 more minutes. Set aside the pork again, boil the sauce down to a gravy and add the balsamic vinegar and garlic powder. Pour the sauce over the chops and serve.

Serves 2 to 4, depending on the size of the chops.

PORK CHOPS WITH TROPICAL FRUIT

If you like fruit and meat, you'll love this dish.

½ cup orange liqueur

½ cup water

½ cup chopped dried plums (prunes)

½ cup chopped dried apricots

2 tablespoons lemon juice

1½ teaspoons grated lemon zest (optional)

1 cinnamon stick

⅓ cup chopped fresh mango

⅓ cup chopped fresh papaya

1 tablespoon brown sugar

8 to 10 pork chops

Salt and pepper, to taste

Combine liqueur, water, dried fruit, lemon juice, zest, and cinnamon stick in a medium saucepan over medium heat. Cook until fruits are tender and mixture thickens slightly, about 20 minutes. Remove from heat and stir in mango, papaya, and brown sugar.

Season pork chops with salt and pepper and fry in large heavy pan until browned on both sides and cooked through. Serve with fruit sauce.

Serves 8.

2 Clever Cooks

RICE AND SAUSAGE HASH

This makes a quick one-dish meal. If you are using leftover rice, it's usually a bit dry, so add a bit of water with the rice to help it plump up.

1 medium onion, chopped
4 cloves garlic, minced
1 red bell pepper, chopped
1 yellow bell pepper, chopped
1 bunch kale, finely sliced
½ pound smoked garlic sausage, chopped
¼ cup chopped sundried tomatoes
1½ cups cooked rice
Salt and pepper, to taste

Sauté onion, garlic, peppers, and kale together until onion is soft. Add the rest of the ingredients and cook a few more minutes to warm everything through. Season with salt and pepper to taste.

Serves 2.

PEROGIES

These make a great side dish, but can also be served as the main dish. We like to serve them with bacon and caramelized onions on top, and some fried sausage alongside.

FILLING:

4 slices bacon, sliced into ½-inch pieces

½ medium onion, chopped

1 pound potatoes, cooked and mashed

Salt and pepper, to taste

DOUGH:

1¾ cups white rice flour

1 cup sweet rice flour

½ cup potato starch

¼ cup tapioca starch

1 tablespoon egg replacer

2 teaspoons xanthan gum

½ teaspoon salt

¼ teaspoon garlic powder

1⅔ cups warm water

⅓ cup oil

Fry the bacon and onion together until bacon is crisp and onion is soft. Mix this (including the grease) with the mashed potatoes. Add salt and pepper to taste.

Mix together all dough ingredients in a large bowl until they come together into a soft dough. Roll out on a greased table (we use oil instead of flour, it seems to stick less) into a ¼-inch thick rectangle. We like to cut it into squares about 4-inches wide. Put a small spoonful of filling into the middle and fold the dough over to cover the filling. Pinch the edges until they are securely sealed. Cook the perogies in boiling water for a few minutes, until they float, and then drain on a rack. You can serve at this point, or freeze or refrigerate them for later cooking. We like to finish them by frying them up in lots of butter or margarine until they are brown and crisp on both sides. If you choose to freeze or refrigerate, you need to boil the perogies until they float after taking them out of the fridge or freezer. Again, you can serve them just boiled, or fry them until crisp.

Serves 4 to 6.

EMPANADAS

These are soooooo good! For this recipe, we were forced to be creative and use different flour choices because of what we happened to have at the time. It turned out to be a very good thing. The pastry is more tender if you use butter, and a little more crisp if you use shortening.

You can try other fillings as you like. We've done sweet ones by using apples or cherries, brushing the top with rice milk, and sprinkling with sugar.

DRY INGREDIENTS:

1 cup white rice flour

1 cup potato starch

1 cup corn starch

½ cup potato flour

½ cup sweet rice flour

1 tablespoon sugar

1 tablespoon xanthan gum

1 cup cold butter or shortening, cut into 16 pieces

1½ cups ice water

FILLING:

1 pound ground chicken

1 green onion, finely chopped

2 handfuls cilantro, finely chopped

½ teaspoon ground cumin

½ teaspoon ground coriander

½ teaspoon salt

½ teaspoon pepper

½ teaspoon smoked paprika (use regular if you can't find smoked)

Mix together dry ingredients in a food processor. Add butter or shortening and pulse a few times until you have pea-sized bits of fat. If you don't have a food processor, you can use a pastry blender or a couple of knives. Dump the mixture into a bowl and add the ice water. Mix until it holds together; then shape into a disc shape with your hands, wrap with plastic wrap, and chill for 30 minutes. For the filling, mix all ingredients together thoroughly. Roll out dough and cut out circles (about 3½-inches across). Put about a teaspoon of filling in the center, fold to enclose the filling and seal the edges by pressing with the tip of a fork. You can freeze these at this point, or bake at 400°F for 10 minutes or until the edges start to brown.

Makes about 4 dozen.

2 Clever Cooks

MEATLOAF

I never understood why people would bother making meatloaf until I tried this – it's so good! If you're rushed for time, you can skip sautéing the vegetables, as long as they're very finely chopped. It won't be quite as good, but still delicious.

1 large onion, quartered
2 large cloves garlic
1 stalk celery, quartered
1 carrot, chopped roughly
4 green onions, quartered

⅔ cup ketchup
2 teaspoons Worcestershire sauce
2 teaspoons salt
1½ teaspoons black pepper

1½ pounds ground bison, beef, or ostrich
¾ pound ground pork or turkey
1 cup gluten-free bread crumbs or rice flour
⅓ cup minced fresh parsley

½ cup ketchup or barbeque sauce, if desired

Preheat oven to 350°F.

In a food processor, pulse onion, garlic, celery, carrot, and green onions until finely chopped. Fry in a little butter or oil in a large skillet over medium heat, stirring occasionally until vegetables are soft. Mix in ketchup, Worcestershire, salt, and pepper.

Mix together meat, bread crumbs or flour, and parsley. Add vegetable mixture and combine thoroughly. Form into a large oval loaf on a shallow baking pan. Spread additional ketchup or barbeque sauce over top, if desired. Bake in oven for 1 hour. Let rest 10 minutes before slicing.

Serves 6.

STIR–FRIED BEEF WITH ASPARAGUS AND OYSTER MUSHROOMS

We also like to do this as a side dish and leave out the beef.

1 pound steak, sliced into long thin strips

MARINADE:

1 tablespoon Worcestershire sauce

1 tablespoon fish sauce

1 tablespoon gluten-free soy sauce (or use ½ tablespoon more of each of the Worcestershire and fish sauce)

1 tablespoon lime juice

3 cloves garlic, minced

1 tablespoon finely grated fresh ginger

1 large bunch asparagus, chopped into 2-inch lengths

½ pound oyster mushrooms, sliced (shitake would also be good)

2 tablespoons brown sugar

1 tablespoon cornstarch or 2 tablespoons white rice flour, dissolved in ¼ cup water (if desired)

2 green onions, sliced

Mix together marinade ingredients and add steak; let stand for 1 hour in the refrigerator (if you don't have that much time, just let it marinate on the counter while you prepare the rest of the ingredients). Sauté the garlic and ginger in a little oil over medium-high heat for 1 minute. Add the steak and the marinade and sauté for another couple of minutes to brown. Remove from the pan and set aside. Add the asparagus and mushrooms to the same pan and cook for 7 minutes, stirring frequently. Add the beef and juices back to the pan, stir in the brown sugar, and cook until the sugar is dissolved. If you want a thicker sauce, add cornstarch and water mixture and cook until the sauce thickens up. Mix in the green onions just before serving.

Serves 4.

THAI-STYLE MEATBALLS

A totally different take on meatballs.

MEATBALLS:

2 pounds ground bison, ostrich, or beef

⅓ cup gluten-free bread crumbs

3 tablespoons fish sauce

3 tablespoons agave or honey

4 green onions, thinly sliced

2 tablespoons fresh cilantro, minced

3 cloves garlic, minced

1 tablespoon finely grated fresh ginger

1 teaspoon sesame oil

½ teaspoon salt

½ teaspoon pepper

SAUCE:

1 can (14 ounces) coconut milk

¼ cup water

3 tablespoons sunflower seed butter

3 tablespoons minced fresh cilantro

2 tablespoons finely grated fresh ginger

2 tablespoons agave or honey

1 tablespoon fish sauce

1 small red bell pepper, finely chopped

Lime juice, to taste (optional)

Pinch of red pepper flakes, to taste

Preheat oven to 400°F.

Combine meatball ingredients and mix well. Roll into 1½-inch balls and place on a lightly greased cookie sheet. Bake 18 to 20 minutes, until nicely browned and cooked through.

Whisk together sauce ingredients in a small saucepan and bring to a boil. Simmer while meatballs cook until sauce starts to thicken. You can put the meatballs into a casserole dish and pour the sauce over to serve or serve the sauce separately and let everyone take as much as they want. We like to serve this with rice and steamed veggies.

Makes about 3 dozen meatballs.

2 Clever Cooks

LAMB CURRY

This a good dish to simmer away for a couple of hours, or all day in a slow-cooker.

2 pounds lamb, cut into 1-inch cubes

1 medium onion, chopped

4 cups chicken broth

2 tablespoons curry powder

2 tablespoons ketchup

2 bay leaves

1 clove garlic, minced

1 tablespoon cornstarch or 2 tablespoons white rice flour, dissolved in ¼ cup water (if desired)

Sauté the lamb and onion in a little oil over medium-high heat until meat is browned and onions are soft. Stir in the rest of the ingredients and bring to a boil. Reduce heat to low and simmer for 2 hours, stirring occasionally. If you want a thicker sauce, add cornstarch and water mixture and cook until the sauce thickens up. Serve with rice.

Serves 6.

FISH STICKS

These are especially popular with our kids, but we like them too. We like to use a potato ricer instead of a masher because you get a finer texture, but if you don't have a ricer, just mash them thoroughly.

SALMON MIXTURE:

2½ cups lightly packed riced potatoes

2 cans salmon (skinless and boneless is preferred)**, drained**

⅓ cup brown rice flour

¼ cup ketchup

1 teaspoon xanthan gum

1 teaspoon Worcestershire sauce

¼ teaspoon garlic powder

COATING:

½ cup gluten-free bread crumbs

Mix the salmon ingredients together. Spread ½ of the bread crumbs on the counter in an 8 by 12-inch rectangle. Pat the salmon mixture down evenly on top of the crumbs. Sprinkle the remaining crumbs over the top and pat into the salmon. Cut into sticks of whatever size you prefer. Fry in a little oil in a non-stick pan over medium heat until brown on both sides.

Serves 4.

THAI SALMON PATTIES

These are great for a quick lunch. We gave ranges for the curry paste and lime juice in the sauce, so start with the smaller amounts and adjust to your taste. Because there is no egg in them, they are more delicate than typical fish patties, so handle them carefully.

½ cup coconut milk

1 teaspoon Thai red curry paste

1 green onion, sliced

2 cans salmon, drained

½ cup gluten-free bread crumbs

1 tablespoon lime juice

½ teaspoon xanthan gum

Pepper, to taste

Coating:

½ cup gluten-free bread crumbs

½ teaspoon salt

¼ teaspoon pepper

Sauce:

1 cup coconut milk

½ cup chicken broth

1 to 2 tablespoons lime juice

1 to 2 teaspoons Thai red curry paste

2 tablespoons fresh cilantro, chopped

Mix together the coconut milk, curry paste, and green onion in a small saucepan over medium heat until the curry paste is dissolved. Remove from heat; add the salmon, bread crumbs, lime juice, xanthan gum, and pepper. Mix together the coating ingredients in a shallow bowl. Form the salmon mixture into small patties (add more bread crumbs if the mixture is too loose). Coat the patties with the bread crumbs, then place on a tray to cool in the fridge for 30 minutes or more.

Mix the coconut milk, chicken broth, lime juice, and curry paste together over medium heat until boiling; turn down to a simmer while you cook the patties (this makes a fairly runny sauce). Add the cilantro just before serving. Heat a little oil in a non-stick frying pan or griddle over medium heat; add the patties and cook until browned on both sides, about 4 minutes per side. Serve with sauce.

Makes about 10 small (3 to 4-inch) patties.

2 Clever Cooks

MACARONI GRATIN WITH OLIVES

This is a simple dish to make (especially if you buy olives that are already pitted). If you're in a hurry, you can skip the baking step (and the topping) and just have it as a warm pasta salad. The garlic is a lot stronger that way, so if you're not a big fan of raw garlic, you may want to use less of it, or use roasted garlic instead. This is completely vegan if you use veggie broth.

1 package (12 ounces) of rice macaroni

2 tablespoons extra virgin olive oil

2½ cups chopped Roma tomatoes

1 can beans, drained (kidney, black, adzuki, whatever you like)

¾ cup pitted Kalamata olives, chopped

¾ cup broth (veggie or chicken)

½ cup fresh basil leaves, roughly torn

2 to 4 large cloves garlic, minced

Salt and pepper, to taste

TOPPING:

¾ cup gluten-free bread crumbs

1 teaspoon oregano

1 teaspoon thyme

½ teaspoon salt

¼ teaspoon pepper (or red pepper flakes if you want it spicier)

Preheat oven to 400°F.

Cook the macaroni a couple minutes less than package directions (it should be slightly undercooked – unless you're just going to eat as pasta salad, in which case, cook to your liking). Drain and toss with the olive oil. Transfer to a 9 by 12-inch baking pan. Add everything else (except the topping) and mix well. Mix topping ingredients together well. Sprinkle the topping mixture over the macaroni and drizzle with a little more olive oil. Bake for 20 to 25 minutes until the top is golden brown.

Serves 6.

2 Clever Cooks

VEGETARIAN LASAGNA

This was inspired by the Veggie Lasagna recipe from Looneyspoons by Janet and Greta Podleski. We tweaked it to our liking, replaced the cheese with our "cream" sauce, and found it to be really good. This is a good one to double and freeze the second dish. It's only completely vegetarian if you leave out the anchovy paste (which you can usually find in the dairy section of the grocery store). If you can have cheese, sprinkle some on top after removing the foil.

VEGETABLES:

1 medium onion, chopped

2 cups sliced mushrooms

2 medium carrots, chopped

1 red bell pepper, chopped

1 medium zucchini, halved lengthwise and sliced

3 cloves garlic, minced

SAUCE INGREDIENTS:

1 can (28 ounces) diced tomatoes

1 can (14 ounces) tomato sauce

1 can (5½ ounces) tomato paste

2 teaspoons dried basil

2 teaspoons dried oregano

2 teaspoons brown sugar or agave

1 teaspoon anchovy paste (optional)

Salt and pepper, to taste

1 large eggplant, sliced lengthwise into ¼-inch slices

Salt and pepper, to taste

9 rice lasagna noodles

2 cups "Cream" Sauce (page 40) – made using 1 cup broth and ⅔ cup wine

1 bag (10 ounces) spinach, chopped very fine in a food processor

1 small bunch basil (leaves only), chopped very fine with the spinach

Sauté vegetables in a large pot with a little oil until soft, and liquid has evaporated. Add sauce ingredients, stir, and simmer for 15 to 20 minutes. Season the eggplant with salt and pepper, then sauté in a little oil over medium-high heat until browned on both sides. Boil the noodles until bending in half, but not cooked all the way through. Place in cold water until you are ready to assemble. Mix together the "cream" sauce, spinach, and basil.

Preheat oven to 375° F.

Cover the bottom of a 9 by 12-inch pan with about a cup of sauce (just barely covered). Place 3 noodles on top, then a third of the remaining sauce, half of the cream mixture, then all of the eggplant. Cover with 3 more noodles, another third of the sauce, and half of the cream mixture. Top with 3 more noodles and the remaining sauce. Cover with foil and bake for 30 minutes; uncover and bake another 10 to 15 minutes, or until bubbling. Let sit for 15 minutes before slicing.

Serves 8 to 10.

FRIED POTATO POCKETS

These make a great main dish, but can also be served as a side dish. Choose whichever filling you're in the mood for.

2 pounds potatoes, peeled and quartered

2 tablespoons fine dry gluten-free bread crumbs

1 tablespoon potato starch

1½ teaspoons egg replacer

1 teaspoon salt

MEXICAN FILLING:

1 pound ground beef or bison

1 medium onion, chopped

1 tablespoon taco spice mix

½ cup finely chopped red bell pepper

½ cup grated sheep or soy cheese (optional)

INDIAN FILLING:

2 cups cauliflower florets, chopped into 1-inch pieces

1 medium onion, chopped

1 clove garlic, minced

1 tablespoon finely grated fresh ginger

1 tablespoon curry powder

1 teaspoon ground cumin

1 teaspoon ground coriander

Salt, to taste

1 tablespoon lemon juice

Boil the potatoes for 10 to 15 minutes, or until tender. Drain and press potatoes through a potato ricer (or mash thoroughly). Mix in the bread crumbs, potato starch, egg replacer, and salt. If the mixture is too dry (it shouldn't crack when flattened) add 1 tablespoon rice milk and ½ tablespoon potato starch at a time until the desired consistency is reached.

FOR THE MEXICAN FILLING:

Fry the beef and onion with spice mix until browned and cooked through. Take off the heat and let cool to room temperature; mix in the red pepper and cheese.

FOR THE INDIAN FILLING:

Fry everything except the lemon juice and cook, covered until the cauliflower is tender. Add a little water to keep everything from sticking and to help the cauliflower cook faster. Take off the heat and mix in the lemon juice.

Grab a mandarin orange-sized piece of the potato mixture. Make an indentation with your thumb and press the dough into a cup-like shape, making sure that the dough is an even ¼-inch thickness. Fill the hole you've made with your filling and work the edges together to seal. Flatten gently into a patty about ¾-inch thick. Deep fry in hot oil about 5 minutes total, turning halfway through, or pan fry in shallow oil until golden brown, about 5 minutes per side.

Makes about nine 3½-inch patties.

2 Clever Cooks

BAKING

FINALLY FANTASTIC BREAD

This is amazing gluten-free and rice-free bread. It's worth buying a bread machine for – you'll probably be making it a couple of times a week after you taste it. It does seem to vary a bit each time you make it – bread is a bit finicky depending on a lot of different factors, but it is still always better than any gluten-free bread we've ever bought in a store. We've included instructions for both a bread machine and a mixer; use whichever you have.

WET INGREDIENTS:

1½ cups warm water

3 tablespoons olive oil

3 tablespoons agave or honey

2 teaspoons apple cider vinegar

DRY INGREDIENTS:

¾ cup sorghum flour

⅔ cup potato starch

⅓ cup amaranth flour

⅓ cup millet flour

⅓ cup arrowroot or cornstarch

⅓ cup finely ground flax seed

1 tablespoon egg replacer

2½ teaspoons xanthan gum

2 teaspoons yeast (we've used both instant and active dry and they both work fine)

1½ teaspoons salt

½ cup hemp seeds

½ cup sunflower or pumpkin seeds (optional)

BREAD MAKER INSTRUCTIONS:

Place wet ingredients in the bottom of your bread machine. Mix the dry ingredients well and add to the bread machine. Set for a regular loaf, medium crust (keep in mind that all bread machines are different, so if it seems under baked, try the large loaf setting the next time). Listen for the end of the first kneading cycle and then, with a wet hand, reach in and remove the paddle. Smooth the top with a wet rubber spatula. If you can't wait around for the end of the first kneading cycle, don't worry about taking out the paddle; the bread will still be fine, but will have a hole in the bottom from the paddle.

MIXER INSTRUCTIONS:

Mix the wet ingredients on low speed. Stop the mixer, add the dry ingredients, and mix again on low speed for 30 seconds or so. Scrape down the sides of the bowl and mix for 4 minutes at medium speed. Scrape the batter into a well greased 9 by 5-inch loaf pan and let rise in a warm place for 60 to 90 minutes, until the dough reaches the top of the pan. Bake in a preheated 350°F oven for 60 to 70 minutes, or until the loaf easily pops out after running a knife along the sides of the pan. If it doesn't come out of the pan easily after running a knife around the sides, it's not done; let it bake another 10 minutes or so.

Makes 1 loaf.

"WHITE" BREAD

This is for those of you who prefer white bread. It has a moist and chewy texture with a crisp crust. We've included instructions for both a bread machine and a mixer; use whichever you have.

WET INGREDIENTS:

2 cups warm water

¼ cup oil

¼ cup agave or honey

2 teaspoons apple cider vinegar

DRY INGREDIENTS:

2 cups brown rice flour

½ cup tapioca starch

¼ cup amaranth flour

¼ cup potato flour (NOT potato starch)

1 tablespoon egg replacer

1 tablespoon xanthan gum

1 tablespoon instant yeast

1 teaspoon salt

BREAD MAKER INSTRUCTIONS:

Add the wet ingredients into the bread machine. Mix the dry ingredients well and add to the bread machine. Set the bread maker to large loaf, medium crust (or use the gluten-free cycle if it has one). Scrape down the sides of the pan with a rubber spatula occasionally for the first couple of minutes of mixing to make sure everything is well incorporated. Listen for the end of the first kneading cycle and then, with a wet hand, reach in and remove the paddle. Smooth the top with a wet rubber spatula. If you can't wait around for the end of the first kneading cycle, don't worry about taking out the paddle; the bread will still be fine, but it will have a hole in the bottom from the paddle.

MIXER INSTRUCTIONS:

Mix the wet ingredients on low speed. Stop the mixer, add the dry ingredients, and mix again on low speed for 30 seconds or so. Scrape down the sides of the bowl and mix for 4 minutes at medium speed. Scrape the batter into a well greased 9 by 5-inch loaf pan and let rise in a warm place for 60 to 90 minutes, until the dough reaches the top of the pan. Bake in a preheated 350°F oven for 60 minutes, or until the loaf easily pops out after running a knife along the sides of the pan. If it doesn't come out of the pan easily after running a knife around the sides, it's not done; let it bake another 10 minutes or so.

Makes 1 loaf.

BASIC BREAD VARIATIONS

Use either of the previous recipes, but if you use the Finally Fantastic Bread recipe, you can leave out the hemp seeds and sunflower seeds, if you prefer.

HOT CROSS BUNS

Use the basic recipe and add ½ cup candied fruit, double the agave or honey, and shape into buns with a rubber spatula on a greased cookie sheet. Let the buns rise for 90 minutes, then bake for 30 minutes at 350°F, or until golden brown.

HAMBURGER/HOT DOG BUNS

Use the basic recipe and shape into hot dog or hamburger bun shapes (about ½-inch thick) with a rubber spatula on a greased cookie sheet. Let buns rise for 90 minutes; sprinkle with sesame seeds if desired (gently pat them into the buns so they stick). Bake for 30 minutes at 350°F, or until golden brown.

PRETZELS

Use the basic recipe and then put the batter in a piping bag (or just a Ziploc-type bag that you cut the corner off). Pipe out in either sticks or the classic twisted pretzel shape. Let rise for 60 minutes; sprinkle with coarse salt and gently press it in. Bake for 30 minutes at 350°F, or until golden brown. You could also leave off the salt, dip them in melted butter or margarine when they come out of the oven, and then roll them in cinnamon sugar.

SAVOURY SANDWICH BREAD

Use the basic recipe and include the following with the dry ingredients:

1 tablespoon dried oregano, 1 tablespoon dried thyme, 1 tablespoon minced fresh garlic or ½ teaspoon dried garlic.

PIZZA CRUSTS

Make the basic white bread recipe, but spread it into two 9-inch circles on parchment paper or a silicone baking mat on top of a sheet pan.

Bake at 350°F for 10 minutes; then add topping and bake until sauce is bubbling. You could also freeze after the first baking for later use.

FOCACCIA

This is nice to have with a saucy dish, or just on its own dipped in olive oil and balsamic vinegar. It is best served warm out of the oven.

DRY INGREDIENTS:

¼ cup rice flour

¼ cup millet flour

¼ cup sorghum flour

¼ cup potato starch

¼ cup arrowroot or corn starch

¼ cup tapioca starch

1 tablespoon sugar

2¼ teaspoons (1 packet) instant yeast

¾ teaspoon xanthan gum

½ teaspoon salt

WET INGREDIENTS:

⅔ cup warm water

1 tablespoon olive oil

TOPPING:

Olive oil

Coarse salt

Fresh rosemary and/or thyme leaves

Mix dry ingredients together using an electric mixer on low speed. Add the wet ingredients and beat at medium speed for 2 minutes. Spread evenly into a greased 8 by 8-inch pan; set aside in a warm place to rise until doubled in size (about 1 hour). Drizzle with a little olive oil, and sprinkle with coarse salt and herbs. Preheat oven to 400°F; bake for 20 minutes, or until golden brown.

Makes four 4-inch squares.

BUCKWHEAT PANCAKES

We love this recipe because it's so simple and quick. It doesn't make a lot of pancakes, so you may want to double it if you're cooking for more than 2 or 3 people. Make sure you use light buckwheat flour. If it's just labelled buckwheat flour, it is probably the dark variety, which is too strong tasting in this recipe.

DRY INGREDIENTS:

¾ cup light buckwheat flour

1½ teaspoons baking powder

Pinch of salt

WET INGREDIENTS:

½ cup water

¼ cup juice (orange, apple, grape - whatever you happen to have on hand)

1 tablespoon oil

1 tablespoon honey or agave or maple syrup

Mix the dry ingredients together. Add wet ingredients and combine. Add more water if the batter is too stiff (it should be thick, but pourable). Fry on medium heat, in a non-stick pan, until lightly browned on both sides.

Makes about 10 medium sized pancakes.

WAFFLES

Thanks to Erin's sister Shae for this easy recipe. They taste just like regular wheat waffles.

DRY INGREDIENTS:

2¼ cups rice flour

4 teaspoons baking powder

1 tablespoon egg replacer

1 teaspoon xanthan gum

¾ teaspoon salt

WET INGREDIENTS:

2¼ cups rice milk

½ cup canola oil

1½ tablespoons maple syrup

Mix the dry ingredients together. Add wet ingredients and combine. Pour into a pre-heated waffle iron and cook for about 5 minutes (this will vary depending on your waffle iron; you may need to experiment a bit).

Makes five 7-inch round waffles.

2 Clever Cooks

CORNMEAL MUFFINS

These are great with chili or pasta with tomato sauce. Serve warm; cut in half and spread with butter or margarine – yum! These are fairly sweet, so cut the sugar down to 2 tablespoons if you prefer.

WET INGREDIENTS:

1¼ cups rice milk

¾ cup cornmeal

¼ cup vegetable oil

DRY INGREDIENTS:

⅔ cup rice flour

⅓ cup sugar

3 tablespoons potato starch

2 tablespoons tapioca starch

1 tablespoon baking powder

1½ teaspoons egg replacer

½ teaspoon salt

Preheat oven to 400°F.

Combine rice milk and cornmeal. Let stand 10 minutes, and then mix in oil. Mix together dry ingredients, add wet ingredients, and stir until combined. Fill greased muffin tins ⅔ full. Bake for 15 to 20 minutes.

Makes 12 muffins.

BANANA MUFFINS

These are very easy and adaptable – add whatever bits you like in a muffin: chocolate chips, raisins, currants, cranberries, nuts, or just have them plain. You could also make it simpler by baking in an 8-inch square pan for 25 to 30 minutes.

DRY INGREDIENTS:

1 cup brown rice flour

½ cup amaranth flour

¼ cup potato starch

1 teaspoon baking powder

½ teaspoon baking soda

½ teaspoon salt

WET INGREDIENTS:

½ cup warm water

½ cup oil

½ cup honey or agave

1½ teaspoons apple cider vinegar

1 teaspoon vanilla

2 medium overripe bananas, mashed

Preheat oven to 350° F.

Combine dry ingredients and mix well. Combine wet ingredients (you can do this right in a 2 cup measuring cup), add to dry ingredients and mix. Add bananas (and any other optional bits you'd like), and stir until everything is combined. Fill greased muffin tins ⅔ full and bake for 25 to 30 minutes, until nicely browned.

Makes 12 muffins.

2 Clever Cooks

CARROT CAKE MUFFINS

If you'd prefer a cake, bake in an 8-inch square pan for 25 to 30 minutes.

DRY INGREDIENTS:

1 cup brown rice flour

½ cup amaranth flour

¼ cup potato starch

1 teaspoon baking powder

1 teaspoon cinnamon

½ teaspoon baking soda

¼ teaspoon cloves

¼ teaspoon nutmeg

¼ teaspoon allspice

¼ teaspoon salt

WET INGREDIENTS:

½ cup warm water

½ cup oil

½ cup honey

1½ teaspoons apple cider vinegar

1 teaspoon vanilla

1 cup grated carrots

½ cup crushed pineapple, drained

½ cup raisins

Preheat oven to 350° F.

Combine dry ingredients and mix well. Combine wet ingredients; add to dry ingredients and mix. Add carrots, pineapple, and raisins, and stir until everything is combined. Fill greased muffin tins ⅔ full and bake for 12 to 15 minutes, until nicely browned.

Makes 12 muffins.

2 Clever Cooks

ORANGE DATE MUFFINS

These are based on Dana's Mom's recipe and are amazing – really simple to make too. They also keep well – for several days in a covered container.

WET INGREDIENTS:

1 whole orange (unpeeled), cut into about 8 sections

½ cup orange juice

½ cup chopped dates

½ cup butter or margarine, softened

DRY INGREDIENTS:

1 cup rice flour

¾ cup sugar

¼ cup tapioca starch

¼ cup potato starch

1½ teaspoons egg replacer

1 teaspoon xanthan gum

1 teaspoon baking soda

1 teaspoon baking powder

½ teaspoon salt

Preheat oven to 350°F.

Blend the wet ingredients in blender until smooth. Mix dry ingredients in a large bowl, and then stir in wet mixture. Scoop into greased muffin tins and bake for 25 to 30 minutes, until dark golden brown.

Makes 12 muffins.

CEREAL DATE MUFFINS

You can use your favourite gluten-free flake-type cereal here – we like Mesa Sunrise from Nature's Path (it's a mix of organic flax, corn, amaranth, buckwheat, and quinoa). These are fairly healthy (no sugar), and not too sweet. You could add some additional dried fruit if you'd like.

WET INGREDIENTS:

2 cups gluten-free flake cereal

1¼ cups rice milk

¾ cup chopped dates

¼ cup honey

¼ cup oil

2 tablespoons ground flax seed

DRY INGREDIENTS:

½ cup sorghum flour

¼ cup light buckwheat flour

¼ cup potato starch

¼ cup tapioca starch

1 tablespoon baking powder

1 teaspoon cinnamon

¼ teaspoon nutmeg

Pinch of salt

Preheat oven to 400°F.

Combine wet ingredients and mix well. Combine dry ingredients; add to wet ingredients and mix. Fill greased muffin tins ⅔ full and bake for 15 to 20 minutes, until nicely browned.

Makes 12 muffins.

BUCKWHEAT MUFFINS

These are not very sweet, so feel free to increase the sugar if you prefer a sweeter muffin. This is a good way to get a few vegetables and some fibre into your kids. If you can't find buckwheat flakes, you can use gluten-free oats.

1½ cups buckwheat flakes
1¾ cups rice milk
½ cup butter or margarine, melted

DRY INGREDIENTS:
1 cup sorghum flour
½ cup brown rice flour
½ cup brown sugar
⅓ cup potato starch
3 tablespoons tapioca starch
3½ teaspoons baking powder
1½ teaspoons egg replacer
1 teaspoon cinnamon
½ teaspoon nutmeg
Pinch of salt

1 cup grated carrot
1 cup grated zucchini
½ cup raisins

Preheat oven to 400°F.

Soak buckwheat flakes in rice milk for 5 minutes. Add melted butter and stir. Combine dry ingredients and mix well; add to buckwheat flake mixture and mix. Add grated carrot, zucchini, and raisins, and stir until everything is combined. Fill greased muffin tins ⅔ full and bake for 20 minutes.

Makes 18 muffins.

BANANA BREAD

A simple, classic recipe.

DRY INGREDIENTS:

1¼ cups brown rice flour

½ cup potato starch

¼ cup tapioca starch

1 tablespoon egg replacer

2 teaspoons baking powder

¼ teaspoon cinnamon

⅛ teaspoon nutmeg

WET INGREDIENTS:

4 medium overripe bananas, mashed

1 cup honey or maple syrup

½ cup canola oil (or melted coconut oil)

½ cup blueberries or chocolate chips (optional)

Preheat oven to 350°F.

Mix the dry ingredients together. Add wet ingredients and combine. Spoon batter into a greased loaf pan and bake for 60 minutes, or until toothpick inserted into centre comes out clean.

Makes 1 loaf.

LEMON POPPY SEED LOAF

A classic, done allergy-free.

DRY INGREDIENTS:

½ cup brown rice flour

½ cup sorghum flour

¼ cup millet flour

2 tablespoons arrowroot or cornstarch

2 tablespoons tapioca starch

2 tablespoons poppy seeds

2 teaspoons baking powder

2 teaspoons egg replacer

¾ teaspoon xanthan gum

WET INGREDIENTS:

¾ cup rice milk

½ cup maple syrup

¼ cup sugar

¼ cup oil

1 teaspoon lemon extract

1 teaspoon vanilla

Preheat oven to 350°F.

Mix together dry ingredients on low speed in a mixer. Add wet ingredients and mix at medium speed until batter is smooth. Pour into a greased 9 by 5-inch loaf pan; bake for 40 minutes, or until toothpick inserted into centre comes out clean. Good with the citrus glaze on page 99.

Makes 1 loaf.

BASIC YELLOW CAKE

This is a nice basic recipe for a birthday cake. It is quite firm and works well if you want to cut it into shapes or stack it. It doesn't rise very high, so do multiple layers if you want a tall cake.

DRY INGREDIENTS:

1 cup white rice flour

1 cup sorghum flour

½ cup millet flour (sift it to remove the chunky bits if it's coarse)

¼ cup arrowroot or cornstarch

¼ cup tapioca starch

1½ tablespoons baking powder

1½ teaspoons xanthan gum

½ teaspoon salt

WET INGREDIENTS:

1½ cups rice milk

1 cup maple syrup

½ cup canola oil

1 tablespoon vanilla

Preheat oven to 350°F.

Mix together dry ingredients on low speed in a mixer. Add wet ingredients and mix at medium speed until batter is smooth. Cover bottom of two 8-inch round cake pans, or one 9 by 12-inch pan, with waxed paper. Spoon batter into pan(s); bake for 25 to 30 minutes, or until toothpick inserted into centre comes out clean.

Makes two 8-inch round or one 9 by 12-inch cake.

DOUBLE CHOCOLATE BANANA BUNDT CAKE

This cake is moist and dense – nobody will ever guess it's gluten-free! If you don't have a food processor, use a blender for the wet ingredients, or chop the zucchini and pineapple into a fine mince. Otherwise, the cake won't be as smooth and moist. Taste a bit of the skin on the zucchini before grating; sometimes it can be bitter. If it is, peel the zucchini before grating.

WET INGREDIENTS:

1 cup brown sugar

½ cup white sugar

⅓ cup oil

1 medium overripe banana, mashed

¼ cup rice milk

1 teaspoon vanilla

½ teaspoon lemon juice

2 cups grated zucchini

½ cup crushed pineapple

DRY INGREDIENTS:

1⅓ cups brown rice flour

½ cup potato starch

⅓ cup cocoa

¼ cup tapioca starch

1 tablespoon egg replacer

1½ teaspoons baking powder

1½ teaspoons baking soda

1 teaspoon xanthan gum

⅓ cup chocolate chips

Preheat oven to 350° F.

Mix wet ingredients in a food processor until smooth. Add zucchini, pineapple, and dry ingredients; process until combined. Stir in chocolate chips. Spoon batter into a greased bundt pan. Bake for 40 to 45 minutes, or until toothpick inserted into centre comes out clean. Cool for 5 to 10 minutes in the pan before turning it out onto a rack to finish cooling. This keeps well for several days at room temperature.

Makes 1 bundt cake.

CHOCOLATE CAKE

This cake rises beautifully and stays moist for at least 2 days. It is not overly sweet, so it's good with frosting or chocolate mousse (page 102).

DRY INGREDIENTS:

1 cup brown sugar

½ cup cocoa

½ cup potato starch

¼ cup tapioca starch

¼ cup brown rice flour

¼ cup sorghum flour

2 teaspoons ground flax seed

1¼ teaspoons baking soda

1 teaspoon xanthan gum

½ teaspoon salt

WET INGREDIENTS:

⅔ cup warm water

½ cup rice milk

⅓ cup canola oil

2 tablespoons balsamic vinegar

2 teaspoons vanilla

Preheat oven to 350°F.

Mix together dry ingredients on low speed in a mixer. Add wet ingredients and combine on low speed. Then increase speed to medium and mix for 2 minutes. Grease a 9-inch springform pan, pour in batter, and bake for 35 to 40 minutes. Let cool on a rack before releasing from the pan.

Makes one 9-inch cake.

2 Clever Cooks

QUICK CHOCOLATE OR CAROB FROSTING

This one is very quick, sugar-free, and can be chocolate-free if you use carob powder.

1 cup honey

1 cup butter or margarine, softened

1 cup cocoa or carob powder

Combine all ingredients in food processor or mixer until smooth.

QUICK VANILLA FROSTING

2 cups icing sugar

2 tablespoons rice milk or water

1 tablespoon butter or margarine, softened

1 teaspoon vanilla

Beat together until smooth.

CITRUS GLAZE

1 tablespoon lemon, lime, or orange juice

1 cup icing sugar

Mix together until smooth.

COCONUT FROSTING

1 cup coconut milk

1 cup sugar

½ cup butter or margarine

1 teaspoon vanilla

1½ cups unsweetened coconut

Mix coconut milk, sugar, butter, and vanilla together in a small saucepan over medium heat. Cook for 15 minutes (it should boil gently). Add the coconut and stir. Let cool slightly before spreading on cake (it firms up while it cools).

2 Clever Cooks

COCONUT "CHEESECAKE" WITH BERRY SAUCE

This is not like your typical dense cheesecake – it's much lighter. Use whichever berries you like best, or try it with mangos for a more tropical taste.

CRUST:

1 cup brown rice flour

½ cup unsweetened coconut

¼ cup maple syrup

2 tablespoons oil

Pinch of salt

FILLING:

1 can (14 ounces) coconut milk

¾ cup mango juice

½ cup sugar

2 teaspoons vanilla

6 teaspoons gelatin

1 cup water

BERRY SAUCE:

3 cups fresh or frozen berries of your choice

½ cup to 1 cup sugar (depending on the sweetness of the berries)

¼ cup cold water

2 tablespoons cornstarch or tapioca starch

Preheat oven to 350°F.

Mix the crust ingredients together (it will be crumbly) and press firmly into the bottom of a lightly greased 9-inch springform pan (you can also use a pie or tart pan). Prick the bottom a few times with a fork. Bake for approximately 20 minutes, until it starts to brown. Let cool before adding filling.

Blend the coconut milk, mango juice, sugar, and vanilla in blender until the sugar is dissolved. Put in the fridge to chill for 30 minutes. After the 30 minutes, sprinkle the gelatin over ½ cup of the water; set aside for 5 minutes. Stir in ½ cup boiling water to dissolve the gelatin. Add the gelatin to the mixture in the blender, blend to combine. If the mixture is still really runny, set in the fridge again until it starts to thicken up (20 minutes or so), then blend again before pouring into the cooled crust, and refrigerate for about 2 hours, or until firm. If you're using a pie pan, you don't have to worry if the filling is still runny, it's just a problem with the springform pan as it might leak.

Combine the berries and sugar in a saucepan over medium heat and cook, stirring frequently, until the sugar is dissolved. Mix together the cold water and starch, and then add to the berry mixture while stirring constantly. Cook until the sauce has thickened to your liking (should take no more than a minute).

Makes one 9-inch cheesecake.

CHOCOLATE MOUSSE

This is so simple and really yummy.

1 can (14 ounces) coconut milk

¼ cup cocoa

¼ cup agave

½ teaspoon xanthan gum

Add all ingredients into a blender and blend for about a minute until combined. Spoon into serving dishes; refrigerate for at least 2 hours before serving.

Makes about 2 ¼ cups.

BASIC PIE CRUST

This is a good all-purpose pie crust. Leave out the sugar if you're using it for a savoury dish like a pot pie.

DRY INGREDIENTS:

1 cup sweet rice flour

½ cup tapioca starch

½ cup cornstarch or arrowroot

½ cup potato starch

1 tablespoon sugar (optional)

1 ½ teaspoons egg replacer

1 teaspoon xanthan gum

½ teaspoon salt

WET INGREDIENTS:

1 cup cold butter or shortening

5 tablespoons ice water

1 tablespoon rice vinegar

Mix together dry ingredients in a food processor. Cut the butter or shortening into small pieces and pulse into the dry ingredients until crumbly. Add water and vinegar. Pulse until the dough comes together when squeezed in your hand. Check after each 2 or 3 pulses because over-processing the dough will make it too soft. Squeeze together into a disc. Wrap in plastic wrap and place in the refrigerator to chill for at least 30 minutes.

Divide dough into 2 or 3 pieces (depending on how thick you want the crust - we usually stretch it to 3 crusts). Roll out between 2 sheets of waxed paper, until big enough for the pie plate. Peel off the top sheet, invert the dough over the pie plate, and peel off the waxed paper. Pinch together anywhere the dough has come apart. To bake without a filling, prick all over with a fork and bake in a preheated, 450°F oven for 10 to 12 minutes. The crust tends to crack if baked without a filling, but nobody will know because it will be covered. Cool before filling.

Makes two or three 9-inch pie crusts (depending on how thick you roll them).

COCONUT CREAM PIE

This is super easy and delicious. It isn't as dense as a typical cream pie, so we don't miss the whipped cream topping; it is light enough already. Try the chocolate cream variation too.

1 pre-baked 8-inch pie crust (see recipe on page 103)

1¼ cups water
¼ cup white rice

1 can (14 ounces) coconut milk
⅓ cup agave
1 teaspoon xanthan gum

GARNISH:

¼ cup toasted sweetened coconut (we prefer to use organic coconut, so we toast unsweetened coconut, then toss with about a tablespoon of powdered sugar.)

Bring the water and rice to a boil in a small saucepan. Turn the heat down to low and simmer for about 25 to 30 minutes, until all the water is absorbed and the rice is extremely soft. Place the rice in a blender with the coconut milk, agave, and xanthan gum; blend until smooth. (If you don't have a really high-powered blender, you may have tiny bits of rice in the mixture. You can strain it if you'd like, but we don't find it necessary). Pour into the pie crust and cool in the fridge until set (2 hours or more).

Serve the pie with the toasted coconut on top.

CHOCOLATE CREAM PIE VARIATION:

Add 2 tablespoons cocoa with the coconut milk in the blender. You can use chocolate shavings on top for garnish instead of the toasted coconut.

Makes one 8-inch pie.

PUMPKIN PIE

This should fool your relatives at Thanksgiving – they'll think they're having the real deal.

DRY INGREDIENTS:

¾ cup sugar

1 tablespoon egg replacer

1 teaspoon xanthan gum

1 teaspoon cinnamon

½ teaspoon ground ginger

½ teaspoon nutmeg

⅛ teaspoon cloves

WET INGREDIENTS:

1 can (15 ounces) pure pumpkin

1 cup coconut milk

1 9-inch pie crust (page 103), baked 10 minutes until firm (it will not change colour)

WHIPPED "CREAM":

1 can (14 ounces) coconut cream or full-fat coconut milk (refrigerated the day before)

1 tablespoon agave

2 teaspoons vanilla extract

Mix the dry ingredients together thoroughly. Blend together with the wet ingredients in a blender until smooth. Pour the mix into the pre-baked crust and bake for 30 minutes. Watch the filling, as it may bubble up while baking. If it does, just poke with a knife to collapse it back down.

For the whipped "cream," drain off all liquid from the coconut cream (open it from the bottom of the can, the solid part will be on top). Whip the remaining solid cream with the agave and vanilla in a mixer, on medium-high speed, for a couple of minutes, until it's the consistency of soft whipped cream.

Makes one 9-inch pie.

PEAR TARTE TATIN

This is a simple, yet elegant dessert. Try sprinkling with a little cinnamon before serving.

⅓ cup brown sugar

2 tablespoons butter or margarine

4 firm pears (Bosc are good), cut in half lengthwise, stemmed and seeded

1 9-inch pie crust (see page 103)

Preheat oven to 350°F.

Heat brown sugar and butter over medium heat in an 8-inch oven-proof skillet. Add pears and cook, turning occasionally, until coated on all sides. Arrange pears cut side up in skillet. Drape dough over and tuck in the edges. Bake for 30 minutes, or until pastry is golden brown. Let stand 5 minutes and then place plate upside-down on top of skillet. Quickly flip tart over onto the plate. Serve warm, with vanilla ice cream.

Makes one 9-inch tatin.

PEACH CRISP

To double this recipe, use a 9 by 13-inch baking dish and bake for 55 minutes. Use any combination of quinoa, buckwheat, millet, rice flakes, and rolled oats that you have. Try not to use all quinoa though, as it is quite strong tasting. Don't use all rice flakes either, they're too crunchy. If you prefer apples, just use your favourite apples in places of the peaches.

TOPPING:

1 cup mixed flakes (quinoa, buckwheat, millet, rice, or gluten-free rolled oats)

½ cup brown rice flour

½ cup cold butter or shortening, cut into 1-inch pieces

⅓ cup brown sugar

⅓ cup white sugar

½ teaspoon cinnamon

½ teaspoon nutmeg

Pinch of salt

FILLING:

6 cups peaches, sliced

2 cups berries (optional)

¼ cup sugar

Juice of one lemon

Preheat oven to 375° F.

Pulse all the topping ingredients together in a food processor until evenly combined (the topping should stick together when squeezed in your hand). Don't process too long or you won't have a nice "crisp" texture. (You can also just mix everything together in a bowl with a wooden spoon or your fingers.) Mix together peaches, sugar, and lemon juice in the pie plate; sprinkle with topping. Bake for 40 to 45 minutes, or until the topping is golden brown and the filling is bubbling.

Makes one 9-inch crisp.

BROWNIES

We tried many, many recipes before we finally got what we think is the perfect brownie. You'd never know this is gluten, dairy, and egg-free. The key to this recipe is making sure the oil and cocoa powder are completely emulsified.

DRY INGREDIENTS:

¾ **cup sugar**

⅓ **cup buckwheat flour**

¼ **cup sorghum flour**

¼ **cup amaranth flour**

¼ **cup potato starch**

1 **teaspoon baking powder**

½ **teaspoon xanthan gum**

¼ **teaspoon salt**

WET INGREDIENTS:

½ **cup hot water**

½ **cup cocoa powder**

1 **teaspoon instant coffee**

1 **tablespoon ground flax seed**

½ **cup melted coconut oil or canola oil**

¼ **cup maple syrup**

1 **teaspoon vanilla**

Preheat oven to 350°F.

Whisk together dry ingredients. Whisk together hot water, cocoa powder, and instant coffee until no lumps remain; set aside for 5 minutes. Add ground flax seed, stir and set aside another 5 minutes. Add oil, maple syrup, and vanilla to cocoa mixture and whisk together until completely combined (this is very important – make sure there is no oil on top, it must be all mixed in). Stir cocoa mixture into dry ingredients and mix well. Spread batter into a greased 8 by 8-inch pan and bake for 20 to 30 minutes, just until a toothpick comes out with moist crumbs attached. Don't over bake or they will be dry. Let cool completely (the brownies will stay moist longer), and cut into 2 by 2-inch squares.

If you do overcook these, chop into pieces and soak in hot chocolate or hot fudge sauce until warm and serve over ice cream.

Makes 16 brownies.

2 Clever Cooks

NANAIMO BARS

Yes, that fabulous Canadian treat is equally fabulous without eggs, milk, and graham wafer crumbs (and the traditional custard powder, which we nixed because it's full of artificial colours and flavours). These are a bit of a pain to cut, but they're worth it!

BASE:

½ cup butter or margarine

¼ cup white sugar

¼ cup brown sugar

¼ cup cocoa

1¼ cups gluten-free rolled oats (or buckwheat flakes)

1 cup coconut

½ cup hemp seeds

1 tablespoon ground flax seed

1 teaspoon vanilla

FILLING:

2 cups icing sugar

¼ cup butter or margarine, softened

2 tablespoons cornstarch or arrowroot

2 tablespoons rice milk

1 tablespoon vanilla

TOPPING:

½ cup chocolate chips

1 tablespoon coconut oil, butter, or margarine

Melt butter, sugars, and cocoa together in a small saucepan over low heat, until sugars are dissolved; stir frequently. Mix the rest of the base ingredients together in a medium bowl, then pour the butter mixture in and stir until combined. Press firmly into an ungreased 8 by 8-inch pan; refrigerate until cool (about 1 hour).

Mix together filling ingredients with a mixer, on medium speed, until smooth. Spread evenly over base; refrigerate 30 minutes. Melt chocolate chips and coconut oil together over low heat until smooth. Pour over filling and spread evenly. Refrigerate for about 10 to 15 minutes, until chocolate is just starting to set, then cut into 1 by 2-inch bars. Store these in the refrigerator.

Makes 32 bars.

CHOCOLATE TRUFFLE BARS

These are very rich and decadent. You can cut the recipe in half and bake in an 8 by 8-inch pan if you prefer.

CRUST AND TOPPING:

1 cup butter or margarine, softened

2 cups brown sugar

2 teaspoons vanilla

1⅓ cups brown rice flour

6 tablespoons potato starch

3 tablespoons tapioca starch

1 tablespoon egg replacer

1 teaspoon baking soda

2 cups of any combination of quinoa flakes, buckwheat flakes, millet flakes, gluten-free oats

1 cup unsweetened coconut

FILLING:

1 can (14 ounces) coconut milk

1½ cups semi-sweet chocolate chips

2 tablespoons butter or margarine

2 teaspoons vanilla

Preheat oven to 350°F.

Cream butter, sugar, and vanilla in mixer on medium speed until combined. Mix together the flour, starches, egg replacer, and baking soda in another bowl. Add to mixer and combine on low speed. Stir in flakes and coconut. Press about two-thirds of the crust mixture firmly into the bottom of a 9 by 12-inch pan.

Stir together the coconut milk, chocolate chips, and butter in a medium saucepan over low heat. Cook until chocolate is melted and the mixture is uniform, stirring frequently. Remove from heat and stir in vanilla. Pour filling over crust and spread evenly.

Squeeze the remaining third of the crust/topping mixture into small flat pieces (about 1 to 2-inches in diameter), with your fingers, and place evenly over the top of the filling. Bake for 20 to 25 minutes, or until the top is lightly browned; the filling will still be loose, but will firm up as it cools. Cool on a rack completely before cutting into bars about 2-inches square. Store these in the fridge, as the texture is a bit too gooey if you leave them at room temperature.

Makes 30 squares.

CHOCOLATE TRUFFLE FILLED COCONUT TARTS

We love the chocolate-coconut combination. These are quick and delicious.

COCONUT TART SHELLS:

2 cups unsweetened coconut

¼ cup coconut milk

¼ cup agave or honey

½ teaspoon xanthan gum

TRUFFLE FILLING

½ cup coconut milk

8 ounces good dark chocolate, chopped (or use good quality semi-sweet chocolate chips)

Preheat oven to 350° F.

Mix together tart shell ingredients. Spoon into a greased mini-muffin tin, and press firmly onto the bottom and up the sides of each cup. Bake for 7 minutes, or until golden brown. Let cool in pan, and then carefully pull them out.

Heat coconut milk in a small saucepan over medium heat until steaming. Turn off the heat, add chocolate, and mix until melted. Pour into cooled tart shells.

Makes 20 small tarts.

2 Clever Cooks

SEED BARS

A great snack to have around when you want something quick and nutritious.

⅓ cup honey

⅓ cup brown rice syrup

¼ cup butter or margarine

6 cups mixed seeds (we like sesame seeds, sunflower seeds, pumpkin seeds, and hemp seeds)

Mix the honey, brown rice syrup, and butter together in a small saucepan over medium heat. Bring to a boil and continue to boil for about 4 or 5 minutes. Mix the seeds together in a large bowl, add the syrup mixture, and mix thoroughly. Line a large jelly roll pan (about 18 by 13-inches) with waxed paper. Spread the mixture in the pan evenly, then put another sheet of waxed paper on top and press it down firmly and evenly using a rolling pin. Place in the refrigerator to cool, then slice into bars about 1½ by 4½-inches.

Makes 32 bars.

HEALTHY SEED AND JAM COOKIES

These are Newton-type cookies, loaded with healthy ingredients.

WET INGREDIENTS:

⅔ cup apple sauce

½ cup sunflower seed butter

⅓ cup coconut oil, butter, or margarine

⅓ cup honey

DRY INGREDIENTS:

½ cup brown rice flour

½ cup ground flax seed

¼ cup potato starch

2 tablespoons tapioca starch

2 tablespoons sorghum flour

1 teaspoon baking powder

½ teaspoon xanthan gum

½ teaspoon cinnamon

½ teaspoon ground ginger

CHUNKY BITS:

1 cup gluten-free rolled oats or buckwheat flakes

½ cup sunflower seeds

½ cup pumpkin seeds

½ cup dried cranberries

½ cup raisins

¼ cup sesame seeds

¼ cup hemp seeds

¼ cup of your favourite jam or jelly

Preheat oven to 350°F.

Cream the wet ingredients together in a mixer. Add the dry ingredients and mix until combined. Pulse the rolled oats, sunflower seeds, and pumpkin seeds in a food processor to chop them into slightly smaller bits (this helps keep the cookies from cracking apart). Add all the chunky bits into the mixer and mix on low until combined. Roll out into a 6 by 12-inch rectangle on a cookie sheet. Spread jam down the middle of the rectangle lengthwise (about 2 inches wide). Fold one third of the dough over to just cover the jam, then fold the other side over top of that (you'll have a double thickness of dough on the top, and a single thickness on the bottom, with jam in the middle). Bake for 15 minutes, let cool on the cookie sheet, and then slice into 2-inch pieces.

Makes 12 cookies.

2 Clever Cooks

CHOCOLATE SANDWICH (OR ICE CREAM SANDWICH) COOKIES

Kids love these (adults too!), but they are quite crumbly. If you want ice cream sandwiches, just roll the dough out a little thicker (maybe ⅓-inch), cut into circles the size you want, bake, and then fill with softened ice cream. Wrap in plastic wrap and freeze.

DRY INGREDIENTS:

1 cup rice flour

¾ cup tapioca starch

¾ cup cornstarch

⅓ cup cocoa

1 tablespoon egg replacer

1 teaspoon baking powder

1 teaspoon baking soda

1 teaspoon xanthan gum

½ teaspoon salt

WET INGREDIENTS:

¾ cup butter or margarine, softened

¾ cup agave or honey

1 teaspoon vanilla

FILLING INGREDIENTS:

2 cups icing sugar

¼ cup butter or margarine, softened

2 tablespoons rice milk

1 teaspoon vanilla

Mix together dry ingredients. Cream the butter, agave, and vanilla in a mixer on medium speed for about a minute. Add the dry ingredients and mix on low speed until everything is incorporated. Chill the dough in the refrigerator for at least 30 minutes.

Preheat oven to 350°F.

Roll the dough into 1-inch balls and place on an ungreased cookie sheet. Flatten into a ¼–inch thick disk with the bottom of a glass (use a piece of waxed paper between the dough and the glass so it doesn't stick). Bake for 10 minutes, let cool on cookie sheet for a few minutes, and then transfer to a rack to completely cool.

Combine filling ingredients together and mix well. It should be fairly thick, but spreadable. Spread filling on the bottom of one cookie, and then press another cookie on top. These keep well for several days at room temperature in a sealed container.

Makes 2 to 3 dozen filled cookies.

2 Clever Cooks

GINGER COOKIES

If you like crisp ginger cookies, flatten them a little more and cook until they start to brown on the edges. If you prefer them soft in the middle, cook them until they are slightly firm to the touch; don't let them brown at all. If you cook them until they're crisp, they're great to use crushed for a pie crust. These are very gingery, so if you don't want them quite so spicy, cut the ginger in half.

½ cup butter or margarine, softened

¾ cup sugar

3 tablespoons fancy molasses

DRY INGREDIENTS:

1½ cups rice flour

⅓ cup potato starch

3 tablespoons tapioca starch

1 tablespoon finely grated fresh ginger

1 tablespoon ground ginger

1½ teaspoons egg replacer

1 teaspoon baking soda

1 teaspoon baking powder

½ teaspoon cinnamon

¼ teaspoon salt

¼ cup rice milk

COATING:

3 tablespoons sugar

½ teaspoon ground ginger

Preheat oven to 350°F.

Cream butter and sugar together on medium speed in a mixer. Add molasses and mix well. Mix together dry ingredients and add alternately with the rice milk until everything is well blended and the dough holds together (add a little more rice milk if it is too dry).

Mix together the sugar and ginger in a small bowl. Roll the dough into 1-inch balls, roll them in the sugar mixture, and then place on cookie sheet. Bake for 10 to 15 minutes, depending on how crisp you want them.

Makes 3 to 4 dozen cookies.

COCONUT LIME COOKIES

A different flavour for a cut-out cookie. These keep well in a sealed container for up to a week.

⅔ cup butter or margarine, softened

¾ cup sugar

Zest of 1 lime

3 tablespoons lime juice

1 tablespoon coconut extract

1 cup sweet rice flour

½ cup light buckwheat flour

½ cup coconut

¼ cup amaranth flour

¼ cup potato starch

1 teaspoon baking powder

Pinch of salt

Cream butter and sugar together in mixer on medium speed until combined. Add lime zest, lime juice, and coconut extract; mix on low speed for 30 seconds. Add the rest of the ingredients and mix on medium speed until everything is incorporated. Chill the dough for at least 30 minutes. Roll out to ¼-inch thick. Cut out with cookie cutters and place on an ungreased baking sheet. Preheat oven to 375°F; bake for 8 to 10 minutes, or until just turning brown around the edges.

Makes 3 dozen.

2 Clever Cooks

GRANDMA'S OATMEAL COOKIES

These are based on Dana's Grandma's recipe and are just as good. The original recipe used raisins and dates — we use chocolate chips, dried cranberries, and nuts. Use whatever you like in an oatmeal cookie. Quinoa flakes have a strong flavour, so if you use them, it's best to mix them with other varieties.

½ cup butter or margarine, softened

½ cup brown sugar

½ cup white sugar

¼ cup brown rice flour

¼ cup sweet white rice flour

1 tablespoon egg replacer

1 teaspoon vanilla

½ teaspoon baking soda

½ teaspoon salt

½ teaspoon xanthan gum

1½ cups mixed flakes (quinoa flakes, buckwheat flakes, millet flakes, or gluten-free rolled oats - whatever you can find and whatever you prefer)

1 cup unsweetened coconut

¼ cup (or slightly more) **rice milk or water**

½ cup chocolate chips

½ cup dried cranberries

½ cup pecans or walnuts (optional)

Preheat oven to 350°F.

Cream together the butter and sugars. Add brown rice flour, sweet rice flour, egg replacer, vanilla, baking soda, salt, and xanthan gum. Mix well. Stir in the mixed flakes and coconut. Add water or rice milk until batter holds together when you form a ball. Stir in chocolate chips, cranberries, and nuts, if desired. Spoon batter onto greased cookie sheet and bake for 10 to 14 minutes.

Makes 2 dozen 3-inch cookies.

THIMBLE COOKIES

This was a classic back in our Moms' (and Grandmas') day. They are still delicious today. These freeze well, without the jam.

WET INGREDIENTS:

½ cup butter or margarine, softened

¼ cup brown sugar

¼ cup coconut milk

1 teaspoon vanilla

DRY INGREDIENTS:

¾ cup sweet rice flour

⅓ cup brown rice flour

¼ cup potato starch

2 tablespoons tapioca starch

TOPPING:

⅓ cup unsweetened coconut

½ cup jam or jelly

Preheat oven to 350° F.

Cream butter and sugar together in a mixer on medium-high speed. Add coconut milk and vanilla; mix on low speed until combined.

Stir together dry ingredients; add to wet ingredients and mix on medium speed until well combined.

Roll into walnut sized balls, and roll the balls in the coconut. Place on a greased cookie sheet and make a thumbprint dent in the middle of each ball.

Bake 10 to 12 minutes or until golden brown. Cool on a rack and fill the cooled cookies with jam or jelly just before serving.

Makes 18 cookies.

CHOCOLATE COATED PUMPKIN SEED CRESCENTS

These are similar to shortbread – very delicate. The pumpkin seeds add a little colour and texture. The chocolate is what really makes these cookies great.

1 cup butter or margarine, softened

½ cup icing sugar

¾ cup sweet rice flour

½ cup sorghum flour

¼ cup light buckwheat flour

¼ cup potato starch

¼ cup tapioca starch

½ cup finely chopped pumpkin seeds (do this in a food processor or blender)

COATING:

¼ cup chocolate chips

1 teaspoon coconut oil or shortening

Preheat oven to 350°F.

Beat the butter and icing sugar together at medium speed in a mixer. Add the flours and starches, and mix on low speed until incorporated. Add the pumpkin seeds and mix on low speed until you have a uniform dough (it will be quite soft). You can form the cookies right away, or refrigerate the dough for 30 to 60 minutes to make it easier to handle. Mold tablespoon sized portions of dough into 3-inch logs, bend them into crescent shapes, and place on a cookie sheet lined with parchment paper or a silicone mat. Bake for 12 to 15 minutes, or until slightly browned on the bottom. Cool on the cookie sheet for about 5 minutes, then transfer to a rack to finish cooling. Heat the chocolate chips and coconut oil together in a double boiler (or in a bowl placed over the top of a saucepan of simmering water) until melted and smooth. Drizzle over the cookies and let the chocolate harden. Store in an airtight container. These also freeze well.

Makes 3 dozen cookies.

ZUCCHINI LEMON COOKIES

These are sweet and lemony.

¾ cup butter or margarine, softened

¾ cup sugar

DRY INGREDIENTS:

1 cup brown rice flour

½ cup potato starch

¼ cup tapioca starch

¼ cup sweet rice flour

1½ teaspoons baking powder

1½ teaspoons egg replacer

½ teaspoon xanthan gum

Pinch of salt

1 cup finely grated zucchini

1½ tablespoons lemon juice

GLAZE:

1 cup icing sugar

1½ tablespoons lemon juice

Preheat oven to 375°F.

Cream together butter and sugar on medium speed in a mixer. Stir together dry ingredients; add half to butter mixture and mix on low speed. Add zucchini and lemon juice and mix on low speed again. Add the rest of the dry ingredients and mix until batter is smooth. Drop by rounded tablespoons onto a greased cookie sheet (they will spread a fair amount, so leave a few inches in between the cookies). Bake for 15 minutes, or until cookies are brown around the edges. Let cool on a rack. Stir together glaze ingredients. Add a little more lemon juice if needed to make it a fairly thin consistency. Brush onto the cookies with a pastry brush once they've cooled completely. Store in an airtight container.

Makes 2½ dozen cookies.

2 Clever Cooks

ORANGE CARROT COOKIES

These are based on a recipe from Dana's Mom and are really flavourful. The glaze makes them fantastic.

1 cup butter or margarine, softened

1 cup brown sugar

1 cup sweet rice flour

½ cup amaranth flour

½ cup potato starch

2 tablespoons orange rind

2 teaspoons baking powder

1 cup grated carrots

1 cup raisins

GLAZE:

1 cup icing sugar

2 tablespoons orange juice

1 tablespoon butter or margarine, softened

Preheat oven to 375°F.

Cream together butter and sugar. Add sweet rice flour, amaranth flour, potato starch, orange rind, and baking powder; mix well. Stir in carrots and raisins. Drop by teaspoons onto greased cookie sheets. Bake 10 minutes, or until just brown around the edges. Let rest on the cookie sheet 5 minutes before transferring to a rack to cool. Mix together glaze ingredients until smooth; keep covered until cookies cool. Glaze cookies when cool and store in an airtight container at room temperature.

Makes 3 dozen cookies.

CHOCOLATE OR VANILLA CAKE DOUGHNUTS

So, so good! These are not exactly the healthiest treat, so enjoy them on special occasions. They come out extremely crispy on the outside at first, so it's best to eat them after they've sat in a sealed container for a couple of hours and the crust has softened somewhat. They will still have a little crunch on the outside. These keep well at room temperature for two or three days. If you don't have a deep-fryer, just use a large, deep pot, filled no more than half full.

WET INGREDIENTS:

1½ cups rice milk

1 cup sugar

3 tablespoons oil

1 teaspoon vanilla (2 teaspoons if doing vanilla)

DRY INGREDIENTS:

2½ cups brown rice flour

¾ cup potato starch

½ cup tapioca starch

⅓ cup cocoa (rice flour if doing vanilla)

4 teaspoons baking powder

1 tablespoon egg replacer

½ teaspoon cinnamon

½ teaspoon nutmeg

Pinch of salt

Oil for deep-frying

Heat oil to 350°F in a deep fryer or deep pot.

Combine wet ingredients in a large bowl. Mix together dry ingredients; add to the wet mixture and stir to blend (consistency should be like a thick frosting). Drop by small spoonfuls into the oil (we like to use a small scoop to get consistent sized balls). Fry for about 2 to 3 minutes total, turning a few times. Drain on a rack placed over a cookie sheet.

Makes 3 to 4 dozen 2-inch doughnut balls.

CHOCOLATE GLAZE

(great on vanilla doughnuts too)

1 cup icing sugar

¼ cup cocoa, sifted

Rice milk (enough to make a thick, but pourable consistency)

Mix together and dip cooled doughnuts in glaze. Let glaze dry before storing in a sealed container.

2 Clever Cooks

YEAST DOUGHNUTS

Yum! These are best eaten the day they are made. If you don't have a deep-fryer, just use a large, deep pot, filled no more than half full.

1 cup lukewarm water
1 teaspoon sugar
1 tablespoon yeast

DRY INGREDIENTS:
1¼ cups rice flour
⅓ cup tapioca starch
2 tablespoons sorghum flour
1½ teaspoons baking powder
1½ teaspoons egg replacer
1 teaspoon xanthan gum
1 teaspoon cinnamon
½ teaspoon salt

⅓ cup sugar
3 tablespoons butter or margarine, melted
1½ tablespoons water

Rice flour for rolling

Oil for deep frying
Sugar or powdered sugar for rolling

Heat oil to 350°F in a deep fryer or deep pot.

Add the sugar to the water and then stir in the yeast. Set aside until it foams slightly (5 to 7 minutes). Mix together the dry ingredients. Beat together the sugar and butter until combined. Add the 1½ tablespoons water and the yeast mixture, and mix again. Beat in the dry ingredients slowly until smooth.

Flour countertop generously with rice flour. Pat dough into a large rectangle on top of the flour, about ½-inch thick. Cut into 2 by 2-inch squares. Blow off excess flour before carefully dropping into hot oil. Turn once and cook until golden brown on both sides. Remove and place on paper towels to absorb the excess oil. Roll in sugar or powdered sugar while warm.

Makes 2 dozen doughnuts.

2 Clever Cooks

NON-DAIRY ICE CREAMS

These tend to freeze hard, so they benefit from being left out for 10 to 15 minutes before eating to soften slightly. Try adding a tablespoon or two of your favourite liqueur to make them freeze less hard. We also love to add fresh, halved cherries (when they are in season) to either of the chocolate ice creams.

COCONUT ICE CREAM

A good, rich substitute for vanilla ice cream.

1 can (14 ounces) coconut milk

⅓ cup agave

2 teaspoons vanilla extract

½ teaspoon xanthan gum

Pinch salt

Mix together in a blender for a minute. Taste and add more agave or vanilla, if desired. Pour into ice-cream machine and follow manufacturer's instructions.

CHOCOLATE MALT ICE CREAM

Tastes just like an old-fashioned chocolate malt.

1 can (14 ounces) coconut milk

1¾ cups rice milk

½ cup sugar

⅓ cup cocoa

1 teaspoon vanilla extract

½ teaspoon xanthan gum

Mix together in a blender for a minute. Pour into ice-cream machine and follow manufacturer's instructions.

DARK CHOCOLATE ICE CREAM

This is intensely chocolatey.

1¼ cups rice milk

6 tablespoon agave

¼ cup cocoa

¼ cup coconut cream
(or just use the solid part from a can of coconut milk)

2 tablespoons canola oil

2 tablespoons orange or coffee liqueur (optional)

½ teaspoon xanthan gum

Mix together in a blender for a minute. Pour into ice-cream machine and follow manufacturer's instructions.

ICE CREAM TOPPINGS

HARD CHOCOLATE SHELL

½ cup chocolate chips

3 tablespoons coconut oil or shortening

Melt together in a double boiler. Pour over ice cream and it forms a hard shell in just a few seconds. You can store this in the refrigerator and just warm it up whenever you need some (either in the microwave or just over some warm water – it melts very quickly).

CARAMEL SAUCE

¼ cup water

2 tablespoons brown rice syrup or light corn syrup

1¼ cups sugar

¾ cup coconut milk (well stirred)

2 tablespoons butter or margarine

1 teaspoon vanilla extract

Whisk the water and brown rice syrup together in a medium saucepan. Pour the sugar in the center and gently moisten (keep the sugar away from the sides of the pan). Cover and bring to a boil over medium-high heat. Cook 3 to 5 minutes, or until the sugar is dissolved. Remove the lid and cook until the mixture starts turning golden (another 5 minutes or so). Reduce the heat to medium-low and stir occasionally until the caramel darkens to amber, another 5 minutes or so. Remove from the heat and carefully add the coconut milk to the pan, whisking to incorporate completely (it will steam and bubble like crazy – long sleeves and a long whisk are recommended). Add the butter and vanilla and stir to combine. Keeps in the fridge for at least two weeks, warm before serving.

Makes about 1½ cups sauce.